SECRET
OKLAHOMA CITY

A Guide to the Weird, Wonderful, and Obscure

Jeff Provine

Reedy Press
PO Box 5131
St. Louis, MO 63139
www.reedypress.com

Library of Congress Control Number: 2021935140
ISBN: 9781681063362

Design by Jill Halpin

All photos are courtesy of the author unless otherwise noted.

We (the publisher and the author) have done our best to provide the most accurate information available when this book was completed. However, we make no warranty, guarantee, or promise about the accuracy, completeness, or currency of the information provided, and we expressly disclaim all warranties, express or implied. Please note that attractions, company names, addresses, websites, and phone numbers are subject to change or closure, and this is outside of our control. We are not responsible for any loss, damage, injury, or inconvenience that may occur due to the use of this book. When exploring new destinations, please do your homework before you go. You are responsible for your own safety and health when using this book.

Printed in the United States of America
21 22 23 24 25   5 4 3 2 1

CONTENTS

ACKNOWLEDGMENTS

To Debbie, thanks for the lift! And to Dennis, thanks for the tips and the pics.

Special thanks to the staff at the 99s Museum; the staff at the 21C Museum Hotel; Lisa Bradley at the Metropolitan Library System; the staff at the American Banjo Museum; Rachel Cates and the team at Orr Family Farm; Steve Coleman; Dale Day and the team at Remington Park; Danielle Dodson; Lisa Escalon and the team at Preservation Oklahoma; Rod Jones and the team at Oklahoma City University; Jody McAnally and Bill Hogan at OKC Farmers Market; Hugh Meade, Lindsey Cox, and Meg Carlile at Factory Obscura; Anne Murray at the Oklahoma Railway Museum; the team at the Oklahoma Hall of Fame and Gaylord-Pickens Museum; the staff at Oklahoma Contemporary; the staff at the Oklahoma State Firefighter Museum; Sean Peel and the Rodeo Cinema; Matthew and Sharyn Pierce at the Monastery at Forest Lake; Chris Puckett; the staff at the Rattlesnake Museum; Chris Salyer; Michael Schwarz and the team at Abandoned Oklahoma; Jenni Shrum and Michael Grauer at the National Cowboy & Western Heritage Museum; Dennis Spielman; RIVERSPORT OKC; Ginny Underwood and the team at the First Americans Museum; Linda Lynn at *The Oklahoman* archives; and Liz Wood at the Oklahoma Governor's Mansion.

Except where otherwise credited, photos are from the author's personal collection.

INTRODUCTION

In 1889, the newspapers proclaimed that Oklahoma City was "a city born grown!" On the morning of April 22, the population of the area was a few families, all tied to workers at the Oklahoma Station rail depot. Cannon-fire at noon signaled the opening of the land to settlers in one of the biggest races in history. By nightfall on the day of the Land Run, the city had more than 10,000 residents.

Yet there were some growing pains. When surveyors marked off town lots, they neglected to make any streets. This meant anyone trying to go anywhere had to walk across someone else's land, a pastime not too welcome when claim-jumpers could set up their own tent on your land and argue that they had been there first. As if these squabbles weren't enough, two rival groups held elections at the same time, giving Oklahoma City a charter and a council that had nothing to do with each other. US marshals took over for the next six months while the Supreme Court sorted things out.

Since then, Oklahoma City has surged, struggled, and surged again. It became the state capital in 1911, much to the city of Guthrie's chagrin, as it had been the capital from 1907 to 1910. The stockyards made the city a center of commerce, and it was one of the prize stops along US Route 66, the Mother Road. Things slowed down after World War II, when urban renewal changed the cityscape downtown forever. Times became even tougher with the oil bust of the 1980s and the tragedy of the 1995 Murrah Federal Building bombing.

Yet Oklahoma City persevered and turned things around, part of a city spirit that makes the downtown Rotary Club the largest in the world. Bricktown's success sparked a wave of revitalization, and the city even gained an NBA team. With OKC on the map, people are taking a closer look than ever at the hotspots that are not so secret anymore.

THE LAND OF THE RED PEOPLE—ALL AT ONCE

Where can we learn more about the Native Americans who make up Oklahoma?

The long-awaited First Americans Museum opened in the fall of 2021. After construction began at the museum grounds in 2006, ownership changed hands from the state to the city, and the Chickasaw Nation stepped in to complete the project to present a complex to showcase Native American culture near the Interstate 35 and Interstate 40 junction, known as the crossroads of America. The grounds have been molded to create a bold earthen outcropping behind the modern architecture of the state-of-the-art museum. All 39 of Oklahoma's tribes are presented inside the 175,000-square-foot facility, along with outdoor grounds to host ceremonies and dances. Exhibits are permeated with multimedia features to explain backgrounds and present firsthand information on items, both in the permanent collection and those on loan from institutions such as the Smithsonian Institution.

A centerpiece of the museum is a room-sized outline of the state of Oklahoma. The walk-through geography lesson shows not only the land, with its native plants and animals showing the diversity of the state, but also the peoples who had been moved to reservations. Through video and audio, the lessons come alive with the sights and sounds of native Oklahoma. Visitors to the museum experience all at once the enormous breadth of culture,

A family-oriented exhibit in the shape of a walk-through pop-up book features stylized animal characters that convey culture and universal values such as community.

Top: *The walk-through map shows Oklahoma's native peoples. Photo courtesy of First Americans Museum.* Inset: *The First Americans Museum glows with the sunset and silhouette of downtown. Photo by Lori Duckworth, OK Tourism*

clothes, lifestyles, music, and languages of the many peoples who were relocated to Oklahoma.

The experiences at the First Americans museum cater to all the senses, with a full-service restaurant that features responsibly sourced produce and game indigenous to Oklahoma. The menu springs from actual recipes used by tribes, revealing their environments and lives with each dish. What and how we eat is a foundational part of who we are, making the experience an opportunity to learn about each other in a whole new way.

FIRST AMERICANS MUSEUM (FAM)

WHAT: A celebration of shared tribal American culture in Oklahoma

WHERE: 659 First Americans Blvd.

COST: $15 for adults, $10 for seniors, military, and tribal members

PRO TIP: Check the FAM calendar for upcoming demonstrations and events.

WASHINGTON IRVING'S CAMP

What was the writer of "Legend of Sleepy Hollow" doing in Oklahoma?

On his way home to New York from nearly two decades spent traveling Europe, Washington Irving met new friends who suggested an exciting new journey to Indian Territory. The American writer teamed up with British adventurer Charles Latrobe, Swiss count Albert-Alexandre de Pourtales, and Indian Commissioner Henry Ellsworth to journey with an army expedition that trekked through the untamed wilderness in a loop from Fort Gibson. They battled their way through the thick post oaks of Cross Timbers forest before turning south to set up a camp alongside what would be US Route 66 a mere 100 years later.

From there, they traveled nearly the same route as Interstate 35. Irving and his companions were in awe of the open Pawnee grasslands of the frontier. Their route took them over swollen creeks with beaver dams three feet high, and they crossed paths with snarling wolves. South of the North Fork of the Canadian River, in what is now Moore, the expedition hunted buffalo, which Irving described as a brown hillock that "stood with his shaggy front always presented to his foe; his mouth open, his tongue parched, his eyes like coals of fire, and his tail erect with rage;

Left: *Although best known for his time in New York, Washington Irving explored the prairie. Photo courtesy of Wikimedia Commons.* Right: *Two historical markers show the clearing where Irving and his fellow travelers camped.*

every now and then he would make a faint rush." There, they turned back to Fort Gibson, going as far as just about anyone did unless they were headed on to Santa Fe, New Mexico. Upon Irving's return to the East, he compiled his journal into *A Tour on the Prairies*, giving the world a glimpse of the land that one day become Oklahoma City.

Near this point, the expedition spotted a wild horse that evaded capture. It was an appearance of the legendary white mustang of the prairies that would never be caught.

ROAD NAMED FOR A FORT NAMED FOR A GENERAL

What does an Oklahoma City street have to do with a town in Nevada?

People too often think of the Unassigned Lands, the lands ceded to the US by the Seminole and Creek Indians after the Civil War, as completely vacant before the Land Run of 1889. Josiah Gregg's Fort Smith-Santa Fe Trail passed through the southern end of today's Oklahoma City on a cutoff that crossed the Canadian River. This west-running trail hit its peak with '49ers on their way to California, and later a military road was installed to run supplies to Fort Reno. Today, traffic still flows on Reno Avenue.

The fort began as a camp for the 10th Cavalry to maintain order as Cheyenne and Arapaho tribes were removed to Indian Territory. In 1876, General Phil Sheridan made the fort permanent and named it for his friend, Major General Jesse L. Reno, who had been killed at the Battle of South Mountain in 1863. Fort Reno became an economic center for the region, so

FORT RENO

WHAT: A cavalry post established in 1874

WHERE: 7107 W Cheyenne St., El Reno, OK

COST: Tour tickets run about $15

PRO TIP: Keep an eye out for lantern-light historical spirit tours—tickets go quick!

Reno, Nevada, is also named for Major General Jesse L. Reno, dubbed so by the railroad superintendent in 1868. To avoid confusion, the community near Fort Reno added an "El."

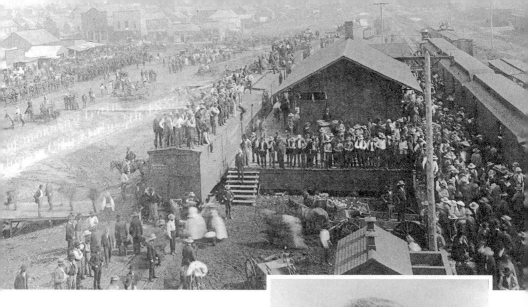

Top: *A look at OKC on July 4, 1889, from long-established Reno Avenue. Photo courtesy of Metropolitan Library System.* Inset: *The man Reno Avenue was named for, Jesse L. Reno. Photo courtesy of Wikimedia Commons*

that even when the railroad came through in 1887, people would disembark at Oklahoma Station to head west. Soldiers rode east along the same path to organize peacekeeping for the Land Run.

Despite its history, there have been attempts to change Reno Avenue's name. In 1933, there was a push to call it "Southwest First Street" to better match the city's numbered system. That fell through, so, in 1952, there was another try at changing just the eastern half of the street. The city held a write-in contest for suggestions. There were 1,800 entries, with everything from "Belle Starr" after the outlaw to the pun-worthy "Nevada," which would have looked delightful on a map. Longtime county commissioner Bob Peebly called the contest off. Numerous people had suggested naming the street after him, but he was satisfied with the existing Peebly Road on the east end of Oklahoma County.

THE FIRST TOWN IN OKC

What's a "boomer," anyway?

In the 1830s, the Five Civilized Tribes of the Southeast were removed in a process known as the Trail of Tears. They were guaranteed the newly organized Indian Territory as a permanent home, but, after the Civil War, the lands were pushed eastward to open up space for new reservations for other tribes from across the nation. Right in the middle was a big block known as the Unassigned Lands. Initially, this had been set aside for freedmen to homestead, but Congress never enacted the bill to do so.

While it sat, a group of land-hungry settlers eyed the Unassigned Lands. According to the 1862 Homestead Act, anyone could claim 160 acres of unused federal land if they improved it. Civil War veteran David L. Payne organized this group, which newspapers derisively called "boomers," because they wanted to boom into the territory. Payne took the name and ran with it. In 1880, he and two dozen others set up a townsite on the southern bank of the North Canadian River at today's Trosper Park. The only problem was that the land was not technically unused; it had been set aside by the government for future reservations.

TROSPER PARK

WHAT: Site of the first boomer settlement in OKC

WHERE: 2300 SE 29th St.

COST: Free park in the south, golfing with reasonable greens fees to the north

PRO TIP: When founding a town, why not put it next to a golf course?

The settlement lasted a few months before troops from Fort Reno chased them away. But the boomers came back, over and over again, with at least four settlements in modern OKC. Each time, they were arrested and forced out of the territory. When

Top: *The landscape of the first boomer settlement, today's Trosper Park.* Inset: *David L. Payne, the leader of the boomer movement.* Photo courtesy of Wikimedia Commons

Payne died of heart failure after a speech, his lieutenant, William L. Couch, took over and led even more attempts at starting a town. Though the boomers never made a successful settlement, they did get the last laugh when the land was finally opened by the Land Run (see "Making the Run" next), and Couch became the first mayor.

The OKC area was largely buffalo-hunting territory, meaning there likely were many nomadic Plains Indian settlements long before the boomers came.

MAKING THE RUN

Fifty thousand people all heading to one spot . . . what could go wrong?

When the Santa Fe Railroad began running through Indian Territory in 1887, it was only a matter of time before the federal government opened it to settlement. In a Gilded Age ideal, it was decided that the land would be given to whoever got there first. A cannon sounded at noon to signal legal entry, and thousands poured across the edges of the Unassigned Lands, hoping to stake a claim on a farm or a smaller town lot. Of course, many people had already sneaked into the area sooner than allowed. For the first few decades in Oklahoma, calling someone a "sooner" was fighting words.

Oklahoma City was estimated to have the most sooners per capita, rivaling Kingfisher to the northwest, as it was already a stagecoach stop. Also known as "moonlighters," they slipped past the largely unguarded Indian Meridian and hid in the bulrushes by the river until they were sure it was past noon. Local rancher William McClure managed to legitimately race the 15 miles in

CENTENNIAL LAND RUN MONUMENT

WHAT: 45 larger-than-life bronze figures showing the Land Run by sculptor Paul Moore

WHERE: 200 Centennial Ave. in Bricktown River Walk Park

COST: Free

NOTEWORTHY: Be sure to cross the canal to see the runners stake their claims.

Oklahoma City was a city "born grown," and it definitely had growing pains, like forgetting to lay out streets. To get anywhere, you had to trespass on someone else's land!

Top: *Like shadows of the past, the statues stand below the Oklahoma City skyline.* Inset: *Enormous bronze statues show the wildness of the 1889 Land Run.*

less than an hour, thanks to having staked fresh horses along the trail before the run; the train arrived about two o'clock. By then, Oklahoma City was already half-settled.

After the reveal of the monument for the Land Run, artist Geoffrey Krawczyk made an addition in protest in 2013 with 39 skulls made of cast iron to represent the event's downside. The land had been hunting grounds for the Osage and Comanche, but it was recognized by the US government as granted to the Creek and Seminole nations, following the Trail of Tears. To ensure the land couldn't be called into question later, lawmakers paid $1.9 million for the two million acres of "empty" land that actually had been populated since time immemorial.

FORTY-FOOT JOG

Why were Oklahoma City streets crooked downtown for 80 years?

Most of the first settlers of Oklahoma City were hoping simply to stake a claim where they could start a home and a business; others had a plan to run the whole show. A group of former boomers organized as the Seminole Land Development Company to start a ready-made city government. Soon after staking their claims, the company went out to plat the town with surveying equipment. It was not long before they bumped into another group of surveyors doing the exact same thing!

The "Seminoles" and the Oklahoma Town Company (later called the "Kickapoos," since hijacking tribal names was in vogue at the time) compared maps and found a dissimilarity. One group had started at the river and worked its way north; the other had started at the railroad and worked west. This meant that the lines they had been mapping out didn't line up. When one side suggested it'd have to toss out the other group's map, guns were drawn. The standoff led to a compromise that they would use one in the north and one in the south, setting Grand Avenue (later Sheridan) as the boundary.

> **FORMERLY CROOKED STREETS**
>
> **WHAT:** Complicated roads based on compromise
>
> **WHERE:** 100–400 Sheridan Ave.
>
> **COST:** Traffic tie-ups for decades
>
> **PRO TIP:** A few streets, such as Hudson and Robinson, are still slightly angled, showing how downtown adjusted over the years.

Oklahoma City started in an era when planners were praising grid designs, and the ground was nearly perfectly flat to allow just that, but a disagreement made the grid crooked.

OKLAHOMA CITY
INDIAN TERRITORY.
1890.

VOTE
CITIZENS
TICKET
NOMINATED
PEOPLE

OKLAHOMA CITY
Election DAY   MAY 1ST 1889

Top: *The famed tin-plate map of early Oklahoma City shows the jog on Broadway Avenue and Robinson Avenue where they meet Grand.* Bottom: *OKC's first elections were highly contested. Photos courtesy of Metropolitan Library System*

Due to the discrepancy, streets had a roughly 40-foot jog of two T-intersections. To get north of old Grand, drivers had to stop, turn left, go a few feet, and then turn right. It was a headache from the beginning, and a nightmare when automobiles came into use.

Fortunately, or unfortunately for the buildings that got in the way, Architect I. M. Pei had a plan to fix it . . . after eight decades! The Pei Plan, carried out in the 1960s and 1970s, was a controversial urban redevelopment plan that resulted in the demolition of many historic structures.

ADOPT-A-POTHOLE

Could people really adopt potholes in Oklahoma City?

Times were tough in Oklahoma City after the oil crash of 1986. As an oil producer during the energy crisis of the 1970s, Oklahoma had been doing fine, with wells opening up all over the state. But when the price of a barrel of oil dropped from its $40 peak in 1981 to less than a third of that five years later, people who had been speculating that oil would stay strong got caught in the lurch. Companies folded, unable to bring in anywhere near the money needed to keep their loans afloat. Without that money coming in, banks that had loaned out millions were suddenly insolvent. Beginning with the famed Penn Square Bank closing on July 5, 1982, Oklahoma City experienced an economic spiral that affected the whole country. The city struggled with revenue, and budgets were reined in. This meant that smaller issues, such as road repair, were pushed to the wayside. Oklahoma City soon became infamous for its crumbling streets filled with potholes.

ADOPTING A POTHOLE

WHAT: Pay to fill in a car-killing pothole

WHERE: All over town in 1988

COST: $10

PRO TIP: The project ended in Mayor Ron Norick's day, but you can still find a pothole or two in OKC if you look hard enough.

In 1988, people could call the Pothole Hotline to put a little cash into making roads better—very little indeed, only $10!

14

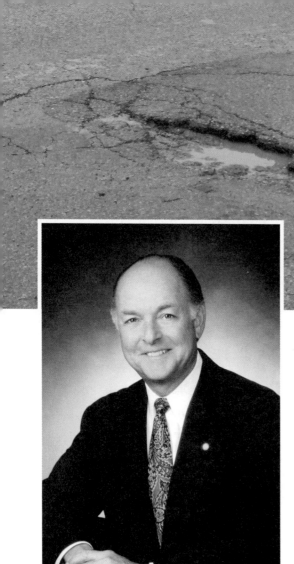

Top: *Legend states that there are a few potholes around town to this day.* Inset: *Mayor Ron Norick, smiling for his official portrait. Photo courtesy of Metropolitan Library System.*

Mayor Ron Norick instituted a plan to fix the problem, at least temporarily. Borrowing from the success of the Adopt-a-Highway program that helped clean up litter, Norick invited citizens, clubs, and businesses to adopt potholes for repair. People could contribute $10 to fill a pothole, or they could adopt an entire block for $100. A pair of disc jockeys in Louisiana thought the project was hilarious and put their money together to buy one. Norick didn't mind; he joked right back that he was glad that OKC could export potholes. He suggested they set up a program with the city of Lafayette to trade potholes for trees one-for-one. Though it all seemed silly, the press did pick up the story, and on a single weekend raised thousands of dollars for roadwork in Oklahoma City.

THE DEATH OF MAYOR WILLIAM L. COUCH

Did OKC's first mayor really die in a gunfight?

Though some people like to argue it, William Couch was our first mayor in Oklahoma City. The problem came with the establishment of city government in the wild times of the Land Run. A few days after, on April 26, 1889, the fellows behind the Seminole Land Development Company said it was time to vote for mayor and a few other offices. People filed into tents, cast their votes, and Couch won, thanks to his years of popularity pushing for Oklahoma settlement. In another election on May 1, he won again.

His term was tumultuous, and it ended suddenly when Couch resigned on November 11. Congress was sorting out local government in the territory, meaning things were getting complicated for the office, specifically that homesteaders had to live inside the city where they were running to be mayor. Couch had staked his claim west of the city limits, taking a larger farm plot while expecting the city to grow. To complicate things further, Couch's own land claim was being disputed by two other homesteaders, who called him a sooner.

Couch spent the next few months working on his homestead. Elsewhere on the 160 acres, two other homes were going up as well. The men stayed clear of each other for the most part until that spring, when Couch ran across J. C. Adams. They

Technically, he didn't die in the fight. Couch was wounded in the fight and died from his injuries a few days later.

THE '89ER TRAIL

WHAT: A walking tour of downtown OKC, featuring historical markers

WHERE: 124 E Sheridan Ave.

COST: Free, just some reading

PRO TIP: Check out 89ertrail.com for a full list of markers.

Top: *Couch's legacy lives on with a street named for him.* Inset: *The official portrait of our twice-elected first mayor, William L. Couch. Photo courtesy of Metropolitan Library System*

decided to settle things once and for all with a duel. Adams won; Couch was shot in the knee. Within a week, his wound began to fester, and he died on April 21, 1890. Oklahoma City held a memorial service on April 22, where thousands paid their respects to Couch while simultaneously observing the first anniversary of a city he helped found.

AN ORIGINAL FARM

What's a frontier farm doing next to the capitol?

Oklahoma City in its first months was, literally, a lawless place. The city itself was in such turmoil, with two rival land "companies" attempting to hold rival elections for different city charters, that it took the United States Supreme Court to sort out who was in charge. After a year of legal vagueness outside of town, Congress created a territorial government on May 2, 1890, with the Oklahoma Organic Act. Even then, there were a lot of disagreements to settle, particularly with many people claiming the same land and accusing one another of being sooners.

Ohio lawyer and newspaperman William Fremont Harn was called by Secretary of the Interior John W. Noble in 1891 to serve as a special agent of the US Land Office to investigate sooners and sort out who properly owned what in Oklahoma. After two years of service, he turned to private practice in the newfound town and officially made it his lifelong home by purchasing a 160-acre farm northeast of town. Mrs. Harn was disappointed when they did not return to Ohio, so William offered her any design she liked in the National Home Builders catalog. Visitors can still visit the yellow Queen Anne-style home she picked, right in the middle of Oklahoma City.

While the farm has decreased in size as Oklahoma City has expanded through the years, such as when Harn gave 40 acres

---

Mr. Harn lived in the house until 1944, and left it to his niece, who deeded it to the city in 1967, so only two generations lived there before it became a museum.

The barn and yellow Queen Anne-style house still stand prominently on Harn's farm.

for the new capitol, the Harn Homestead still offers 10 acres of genuine frontier farmland with six historic buildings. It is a popular place for field trips to see century-old farm equipment and an original one-room schoolhouse. Guides lead tours through the antiques-furnished home with stories of the Harns and their long service to the city. Every fall, the Haunt the Harn festival brings in crowds for trick-or-treating, crafts, old-time games, and a petting zoo, bringing animals back to the farm where they had been when it was in the countryside.

HARN HOMESTEAD

WHAT: A showcase of territorial history with a 1904 farmhouse, a one-room schoolhouse, and museum.

WHERE: 1721 N Lincoln Blvd.

COST: Two-hour program $7 per child, $5 per adult sponsor

PRO TIP: Try your hand at frontier farming techniques!

THE BRICKTOWN CANAL'S PREDECESSOR

What happened to OKC's first canal?

The Metropolitan Area Projects Plan (MAPS) was voter-approved in 1993 to put a one-penny sales tax to work elevating Oklahoma City to the big leagues. The project completed much-needed renovations, but it became most famous for its new additions to the city: a ballpark, a downtown library, and, of course, the Bricktown Canal.

The canal was a vision modeled after other cities' river walks. Construction crews tore out the skid row on California Avenue for several blocks, digging down to create a sunken flow of water adorned with bridges, lights, and flatboats full of curious visitors. It runs for a mile, jogging south under Reno, lolling past the Sonic Drive-In headquarters, and then rounding out in the park at the end of the Boathouse District. It is the center of a more than $100 million investment in what once was one of the worst parts of town.

BRICKTOWN WATER TAXI

WHAT: Enjoy a leisurely cruise down the Bricktown Canal

WHERE: 111 S Mickey Mantle Dr.

COST: $12 regular; $9 youths; $4 child; $10 seniors, disabled, or military

PRO TIP: Park in the River Walk Parking south of Bass Pro Shop for free.

The Bricktown Canal is the quintessential example of successful urban revitalization, but it wasn't Oklahoma City's first attempt at canal-building.

Top: *It took a century, but the dream of floating down the OKC canal has been realized.*
Bottom: *Old blends with the new in refitted buildings from the Wholesale District to the modern Bricktown.*

Yet the canal wasn't the first one in Oklahoma City, not by more than 100 years. The Grand Canal was an idea to bring water in from the North Canadian River and create an artificial stream that would serve as an economic powerhouse as well as a luxury playground. Only eight months after the Land Run, eager residents had invested by digging six miles of canal and constructing a mill and a power plant. Citizens had already purchased boats with dreams of floating on a lazy afternoon.

On December 9, 1889, the dams were broken, and the river flooded into the canal. Amid the cheering, however, it was clear that something was wrong. More water flowed in than went out. Levels started to fall and, by day three, Grand Canal was just a soggy ditch. Despite efforts to save it, the sandy bottom just wouldn't hold water, and Oklahoma City would have to wait another century for a canal.

THE GOLDEN AGE OF RAIL

Where can you ride a historical train in OKC?

People often talk about "living museums" where they walk into a recreated world from the past, and the Oklahoma Railway Museum is an operating museum. Its grounds feature a restored rail depot, the canopy from OKC's historic Union Station, and a host of locomotives, passenger cars, sleeping cars, boxcars, and cabooses. While the equipment is impressive enough lined up on the rails of the yard, the museum goes the extra mile by operating the trains, with guests welcome to join in.

In 1903, the Missouri-Kansas-Texas (MKT, or "Katy") Railroad came through Oklahoma City to crisscross the older, north-south Santa Fe line. Towns up and down the line campaigned for the honor, and OKC won out, to make it the city it is today. On a track from the Katy line going from the museum down to 10th Street before interchanging with Union Pacific, museum trains still run on weekend excursions and for special holiday events. These include the Halloween Train with costume contests, the bunny-led Easter Train, and the popular Polar Express at Christmas with hot

OKLAHOMA RAILWAY MUSEUM

WHAT: An operating museum collecting dozens of locomotives and railroad cars

WHERE: 3400 NE Grand Blvd.

PRO TIP: Free

NOTABLE: Train rides are offered the first and third Saturdays from April through September; book your $12 tickets beforehand at oklahomarailwaymuseum.org.

The Oklahoma Railway Museum has served as location shooting for numerous film projects, including *Bringing Up Bobby* and *The Pale Door.*

Top: *Trains of all kinds line up along the rails at the Oklahoma Railway Museum.*
Bottom: *In addition to trains, the museum shows restored depots and models.*

chocolate, cookies from dancing chefs, and readings from the Polar Express on the journey to meet Santa.

Riding trains is only the beginning at the Railway Museum. Special programs include completing scout merit badge projects, accessing the archives and oral history records, viewing model train displays, hosting birthday parties in the Birthday Caboose, and renting a traveling teaching trunk packed with railroad activities. Older train enthusiasts can even sign up for the handcar and motorcar ride experiences for different ways to get down the track, as well as "At the Throttle," where participants are trained to be engineers on a running steam or diesel locomotive.

MANSION ON THE PRAIRIE

Who was the Father of Oklahoma City?

Shortly after the Land Run, businessman Henry Overholser stepped off the train at the Oklahoma Station. He was already a wealthy man with real estate and ventures in Kansas, but he had dreams of so much more. Overholser began buying up lots and opened business after business: the Overholser Hotel, the Overholser Opera House, and at least eight two-story office buildings. Though he was never mayor, they called him the "Father of Oklahoma City" and even "Uncle Henry" for the boosterism that turned the field of pitched tents into a city. In preparation for statehood, Overholser helped organize the purchase of land for a state fair, which opened a month before Oklahoma actually became a state.

In 1903, Overholser built a 20-room Victorian mansion on the outskirts of the city, all the way out on 15th Street. It was largely a challenge to others to outdo him, and thus make the city grow. The challenge worked, and prominent Oklahoma Citians built up a whole neighborhood of glamorous homes that would become today's Heritage Hills. The Overholsers were the center of Oklahoma City society and hosted events from literary readings to weddings for the who's-who.

Mr. Overholser passed away in 1915, but his wife, Anna, continued to live in the stately home until her own death in 1940.

The spirit of Mrs. Overholser is said still to dwell in the mansion. Her figure, with hair and clothes in 1910s style, can sometimes be seen peeking through the windows.

Top: *The Overholser Mansion still stands in elegance, now a feature of Heritage Hills.* Inset: *Original stained glass near where Mrs. Overholser is said to appear.*

The house was inherited by their daughter, Henry Ione, and son-in-law, David Perry, who worked after his wife's passing to ensure that the home became a museum. As he signed the deed to the Oklahoma Historical Society in 1970, he remarked, "It was Mrs. Overholser's wish that it go to the city or state. She would be pleased." Thanks to Preservation Oklahoma, the home maintains a frozen-in-time glance into high society of 1903 while still carrying on Mrs. Overholser's tradition of entertaining, with hosted events.

HENRY AND ANNA OVERHOLSER MANSION

WHAT: The first great mansion in Oklahoma City

WHERE: 405 NW 15th St.

COST: $10 for adults, $5 for seniors and students. Children under age 6 are free.

PRO TIP: Attend one of the special Mysteries of the Mansion or Scary Tales tours for historical intrigue and ghost stories.

PARKS BY THE RIVER

Where was OKC's first amusement park?

After the turn of the century, the booming frontier town of Oklahoma City needed a place to play. Enter John Sinopoulo and Joseph Marre, entertainment entrepreneurs who had seen success at Delmar Garden in St. Louis. They worked with Charles Colcord to bring a park of the same name to OKC in 1902. West of downtown, 140 riverside acres blossomed with a 3,000-seat theater, racetrack, and baseball field for spectators, as well as a swimming pool, dance hall, and miniature railway for those looking for adventure. It also offered the first beer garden in the city, alongside a wedding chapel that floated atop a little pond. Cutting-edge motion picture technology was added in 1903 to show *The Great Train Robbery*.

Delmar Garden brought big crowds to see the antics of Buster Keaton and a boxing match between John L. Sullivan and Jack Dempsey. It also served adjacent to the town's first zoo, which opened in 1904 after a deer fawn was donated. More animals came, including wolves caught by hand by US Marshal "Catch 'em Alive Jack" Abernathy, and Old Bruin, the largest cinnamon bear in the country.

Unfortunately, those were the days before river controls were installed, and floods wrecked the park. Delmar Garden closed in 1910. In 1923, a terrible flood devastated the city, leaving 1,000 homeless, including animals at the zoo. They had been let out of their pens to run to safety and were re-caught later, prompting the move to Lincoln Park northeast of downtown.

Delmar Garden does live on—as a food truck park! Check out the pavilion and giant bench at 1225 Southwest Second Street.

Top: *Fun times were had at Delmar Garden's outdoor eatery. Courtesy of Metropolitan Library System.* Inset: *Wheeler Park today, across the river from its counterpart a century ago.*

WHEELER DISTRICT FERRIS WHEEL

WHAT: A 100-foot-high ride at Wheeler Riverfront Plaza

WHERE: 1701 S Western Ave.

COST: $6, kids 3 and under free

PRO TIP: Stick around for food trucks and carnival games around the plaza.

Some things have changed in the past 100 years, but not the desire to chill on the waterfront. Right across the river, people at the Wheeler Riverfront Plaza are doing much the same as they did on fun-packed afternoons a century before. It is famed for its enormous "OKC" sign that has delighted social media, and the historical Santa Monica Pier Ferris wheel that underwent a $1 million refurbishment for its new prairie home.

BAUM BUILDING

What was a copy of the Doge's Palace doing in Oklahoma City?

Moses J. Baum may have been born in Mississippi, but he found his calling in Oklahoma City. Moving to town when he was 18 in 1897, Baum was a master salesman. *The Oklahoman* in 1915 praised him as a "pioneer merchant of Oklahoma City" who established "the first exclusive women's garment house in the southwest, there being no similar business in Wichita, Dallas or any of the other cities in this section." Baum touted his sales as "progressive" through lowering prices by minimizing overhead at his stores and passing on the savings. His ads in *The Oklahoman* proclaimed, "Profits are a thing of the past!"

Baum's sales were so good that, in 1909, he secured a lease from Henry Overholser for the northeast corner of Robinson Avenue and what was then called Grand Avenue downtown. His architects designed a department store and apartment building modeled after the Doge's Palace of Venice, complete with stone arches, high windows, and towering cupolas. The Baum building opened to great fanfare in 1910, but his extravagance caught up with him in 1913 with bankruptcy. Though his own store was gone, he continued his success as a salesman, moving on from store to store throughout the South.

The Baum building, along with the Criterion Theater just to the east, was demolished in 1973 due to urban renewal efforts.

Two of the cupolas were saved and serve as decorative stonework on Shartel Avenue at its intersection with 15th and 18th streets.

Left: *The Baum building in its prime. Courtesy of Metropolitan Library System.* Right: *One of the cupolas decorating the Baum building has a new life as decoration near Mesta Park.*

Crooked streets from the early disputes in mapping Oklahoma City were corrected by widening Robinson Avenue by 60 feet, even though it meant losing some of downtown's most iconic structures. In their place, the Century Center Mall was built, but it didn't seem to attract much traffic. Things were remodeled again to office space, and it's now home to the Oklahoma Publishing Company.

PACKINGTOWN

What were the powerhouse origins of Stockyards City?

Oklahoma has long been cattle country. Even before the Land Run, the open prairie was treated as pastureland for ranchers in Indian Territory, and the famous Chisholm, Shawnee, and Great Western cattle trails rolled across from Texas to railheads in Kansas. After the train came through, it was a much shorter trip for folks to bring their cattle to Oklahoma City to be loaded onto trains for the meatpacking plants in Chicago. A few leaders, including Anton Classen and Charles Colcord, asked, "Why not do that packing here?"

A huge parcel of land on the southwest side of the city was laid out in 1910, and economic incentives brought in slaughterhouses, one after the other. Packingtown was born. For decades, farmers brought in cattle, sheep, and hogs to an ever-growing business that created 2,400 jobs in a time when OKC had only 60,000 people. Along with those jobs came businesses to support the industrial sector,

The National Packing Company, the driver behind Packingtown, bought up so many other meat companies that it was broken up by antitrust laws for fixing meat prices.

Top: *The gate into Stockyards City, through which millions of cattle and thousands of tourists have passed.*
Bottom: *A memorial to the cowpokes of history stands in the middle of Stockyards City.*

including hotels for cowboys, agricultural implement shops, and clothiers. In 1973, the stockyards handled 919,280 head of cattle in a single year, to become officially the largest in the nation. Folks liked to joke that coming in from the west, you could smell Oklahoma City before you could see it, which is fine when that's the smell of money.

Though some meatpacking plants have moved on, Oklahoma City's stockyards are still going strong as the largest stocker and feeder market in the world. In addition to its agricultural significance, Stockyards City hosts thousands of tourists for a taste of the West. It offers cowboy-style restaurants, shops for saddles and western wear, and museums unlike anywhere else.

OKLAHOMA CITY'S OLDEST RESTAURANT

Did ownership of Cattlemen's really change hands in a dice game?

After Oklahoma City got its stockyards, cowboys by the thousands came to town bringing in their herds. Old Packingtown was stocked with hotels and bars to keep the visitors housed and entertained. With beef aplenty as well as hungry folks looking for a place to fill up after working either in the plants or the fields, the obvious solution was Cattlemen's Café, opened in 1910 and still serving prime beef to this day.

Of course, the restaurant has had multiple owners in its more than 110-year history. The most famous change-off came in 1945, when owner Hank Frey and local rancher Gene Wade met in a dice match in a smoky room at the top of the Biltmore Hotel. The stakes were getting steep, to the point Wade had invested his entire life savings in the pot, and Frey matched with Cattlemen's itself, betting against Wade rolling a pair of threes. Wade made the roll, and to this day a "33" brand stands in commemoration on the wall of the Hereford Room.

Today, Cattlemen's is a must for anyone coming into town who wants to experience Oklahoma eats, whether it be actor John Wayne or presidents such as Ronald Reagan and George H. W. Bush. Much of the restaurant is the same as it has been, gradually

CATTLEMEN'S STEAKHOUSE

WHAT: Steaks so fresh you can see where they walked off the truck!

WHERE: 1309 S Agnew Ave.

COST: From a few dollars for breakfast to the market-price Presidential T-bone (as named by George H. W. Bush)

PRO TIP: Ask for the lamb fries, but don't ask what they are!

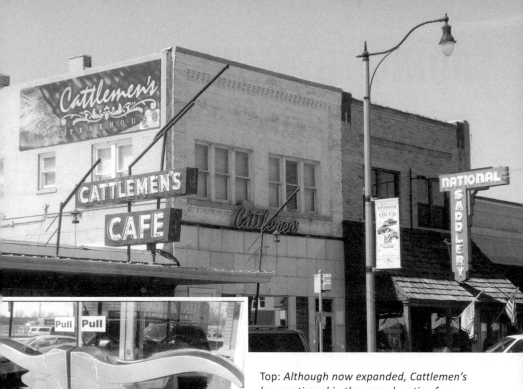

Top: *Although now expanded, Cattlemen's has continued in the same location for more than 100 years.* Inset: *Everything is a reminder of the stockyards at Cattlemen's, even the door handles.*

expanding southward from its original dining room. There's something for everyone with a classic wood-paneled dining room, a brick-walled room with country collectibles hung high, and a western bar upstairs serving up "liquid delights" famous since the days of Prohibition, when Cattlemen's was one of the only eateries in the area to stay open after dark.

Being counted as OKC's oldest restaurant is tricky, but Cattlemen's holds the prize by being continually operated for its many years.

GOING TO MARKET

Where have Oklahoma Citians bought produce for 90 years?

Automobiles changed everything, especially how people bought their food. In times past, people had to grow what they ate, and farmers could bring in extra to small towns a wagon-drive's distance away. When trucks became widespread, farmers started pulling into the big cities from far and wide, and developer John J. Harden made things official in OKC with the Farmers Public Market, built in 1928 at $500,000 (nearly $8 million today) on the site of old Delmar Garden.

In the market's heyday, the open-air docks off Reno Avenue were active all day, nearly every day. Farmers brought in plantings in spring, melons in the summer, pumpkins in autumn, and greenhouse flowers in the winter. Bill Hogan has served as the manager at the Farmers Public Market for more than 50 years, and recalls folks arriving by train with baskets of East Texas tomatoes as big as softballs.

OKLAHOMA CITY FARMERS PUBLIC MARKET

WHAT: A public market each Saturday from 9 a.m. to 2 p.m.

WHERE: 311 S Klein Ave.

COST: Free to browse, but bring your wallet for fantastic deals.

PRO TIP: Check out vendor listings at okcfarmersmarket.com to preorder.

The antique market at the Farmers Market opened in the 1980s, closing in open-air walkways to create a unique place to shop for rare and historic finds.

Top: *The hubbub of street markets in 1910, before the organization of the Farmers Public Market. Courtesy of Metropolitan Library System.*
Inset: *The Farmers Public Market today, still bold in its façade.*

Busiest of all was the two-story Spanish Revival event center. In evenings, the tables were cleared out of the upstairs ballroom for major events. Wrestling and boxing matches brought in spectators, regularly selling out 5,000 tickets at a time. It was the hoppingest music venue for years, bringing in Merl Lindsay and his Midnight Riders as well as Bob Wills and his brother, Johnnie Lee Wills.

The market gained a new chapter when it was bought and restored by Burt and Jody McAnally. Just as their predecessors did a century ago, farmers bring in fruits and vegetables, dairy products, and specialty meats. Local artisans, too, offer specialty soaps, hand sanitizers, and canned goods, while upstairs concerts and special events bring in the crowds. As they say, the more things change . . . .

THE FIRST FIRE STATION IN OKLAHOMA

What's the history of firefighting in the state?

Stepping into the hall of the Oklahoma State Firefighter Museum is like taking a drink from the fire hose of history! It is packed with firefighting tools, vehicles, and mementos from all across the state, including the first-ever fire station in Oklahoma, a small log cabin built at Fort Supply in 1869.

The museum began with a groundbreaking in 1967 and has collected items and stories through its 60 years that will make an enthusiast out of anyone who comes to visit. Exhibits showcase the history of firefighting through woodcut dioramas, fire alarms through the years including an entire alarm room from Enid, and eras in personal firefighting equipment. The extensive Engine Room holds decades of trucks, many with ladders longer than 60 feet, and the horse-drawn Monitor steam fire engine that was built in 1861 and came into service at Muskogee at the turn of the century. Two model horses pulling it are named Sam and Don, after two of Oklahoma City's own firefighting horses, who helped protect the city more than 100 years ago.

One case shows photographs and awards for John J. Lynn, a lifelong firefighter in Oklahoma City. Lynn came to Oklahoma working as a horse trainer for the circus and, in 1908, was hired to serve as the trainer for the growing OKC fire department's horses, the engines of the day. He lived in an apartment above old Station 9, serving more

For additional Oklahoma City firefighting history, contact Station 6 just down the road on Lincoln Boulevard to see relics used by OKC heroes, such as the first motorized engine in town.

Left: *Brought from Fort Supply, the first-ever fire station in Oklahoma was a log cabin.* Inset: *The Engine Room at the Firefighter Museum is packed with the history and progress of firefighting technology.*

OKLAHOMA STATE FIREFIGHTER MUSEUM

WHAT: Exhibits and relics telling the story of firefighting in our state

WHERE: 2716 NE 50th St.

COST: $6 for adults, $5 for seniors, $3 for kids

PRO TIP: Take a moment of reverence at the Oklahoma Fallen and Living Firefighters Memorial and its sculpture, *Just Another Day*.

than 50 years and never officially retiring. According to Oklahoma City firefighter legend, Lynn invented predecessors to the claw tool and double-ended flat and adze Kelly tool some 20 years before the New York City Fire Department developed its own versions. Among his display are examples of his iron entry tools, used to save lives.

FORGOTTEN DOORS

What was the state capitol building hiding for decades?

The Oklahoma State Capitol building went under construction in 1914. Costs skyrocketed due to World War I, so changes to plans had to be made, including postponing the construction of a dome that wouldn't be added until 2002. As years have gone by, construction and remodeling inside have altered spaces as needs changed. Thanks to its convoluted history, no one knows exactly what all is hidden inside the capitol walls.

During a renovation in 2015, crews were shocked while working on the front entry that leads to the Oklahoma marble stairs and legislature rooms beyond. They peeled off thin walling to discover two huge metal doors, 18 feet high and six inches thick. The pocket doors slid along rails into the walls, where they had been hidden for at least 25 years. They were obviously meant to be there; the decorative rosettes on the doors matched the ones outside the House and Senate chambers.

OKLAHOMA STATE CAPITOL TOURS

WHAT: Both self-guided and guided tours show the hotspots of the capitol.

WHERE: 2300 N Lincoln Blvd.

COST: Free

PRO TIP: Call ahead at (405) 521-3356, as guided tours can be limited.

Oklahoma City famously "stole" the capital from Guthrie in a state election in 1910. Among the related legends is that the vote results were announced before polls even closed.

Top: *Murals at the foot of the dome show the energetic and complex history of the state.* Inset: *On display today, the enormous front doors were unknown only a few years ago.*

After some study, state capitol project manager Trait Thompson figured they had been installed during the initial construction, due to fears of war with Mexico. These were days when state representatives were known to carry guns with them in case it came down to an invasion of Oklahoma City from the south. If so, the doors could have been sealed, transforming the capitol into a fortress.

Another round of renovations in 2017 revealed even more forgotten aspects of the capitol. Interior basement walls were opened up to find windows with glass still in the frames. Other walls hid a green-painted door that would have connected offices. With nearly 11 acres of floor space and so many secrets, one can only wonder what else is hidden inside.

DRESSED UP IN TRUSSES

What Route 66 icon is said to be a haunted bridge?

US Route 66 was envisioned as a Mother Road, connecting the middle of the country from Chicago by Lake Michigan to Los Angeles on the shores of the Pacific Ocean. Many bodies of water stood in the way, but Oklahoma City attracted the road by already having in place the Lake Overholser Bridge. It was an example of forethought, just like the lake itself as the first city reservoir, established by a dam in 1916 under the mayorship of Ed Overholser, son of city father Henry Overholser.

The terrible flood of 1923 was kept back only for a few hours by the embankments around the Lake Overholser Dam, and when it was over, the old Postal Road bridge was gone. It was replaced by a ferry for two years while the city built a new, state-of-the-art bridge that has withstood the test of time. At 20 feet wide, 748 feet long, and built in a unique combination of truss styles, it's unlike anything else in the world. When Route 66 came through town a year later, the bridge became an icon that frequently serves in cross-country road trip films. Although a new, even bigger bridge went up alongside it in 1958, the original Lake Overholser Bridge still carries local traffic.

Along with its Route 66 history, the Lake Overholser Bridge also has a spooky legend attached and is known as Crybaby Bridge. The story goes that a mother and child were washed off

Lake Overholser Bridge is one of Oklahoma's many Crybaby Bridges. Another is an abandoned bridge near Kitchen Lake in southeastern OKC at Air Depot Boulevard and Southeast 134th Street.

Top: *The Lake Overholser Bridge has served as the backdrop for numerous movie montages.* Inset: *South of the bridge, the photogenic Lake Overholser Dam has posed for pictures for a century.*

LAKE OVERHOLSER BRIDGE

WHAT: Steel truss bridge

WHERE: 8703-8709 Overholser Dr.

COST: $5 daily fishing license

PRO TIP: Swimming is prohibited in the lake, making for great fishing opportunities.

the bridge in a storm long ago. People walking on the bridge or nearby often hear the loud cries of a baby, even though no one is around. At night, the phantoms may be seen making that final earthly trek at the bridge's edge as a ghostly woman in white with a baby in her arms. Car lights drown out the image, so it's best seen while on foot.

PADDLE THE WETLANDS

What Oklahoma City park is best visited by boat?

At 24 years old, Lee Stinchcomb left Texas on horseback to line up with thousands of others for the Land Run of 1889. He had $35 and a gold watch to his name, along with the horse and saddle that would serve as his transport in the great race to stake his claim for a new life.

STINCHCOMB WILDLIFE REFUGE

WHAT: 1,000 acres of wilderness situated on the west side of Oklahoma City

WHERE: NW 51st St. & N Stinchcomb Ave.

COST: Free

PRO TIP: Visit the Lake Overholser Boathouse at 3115 E Overholser Dr. for small boat rentals to explore upriver into Stinchcomb park.

Stinchcomb rode until he came upon the North Canadian River and made his homestead right along the water. He made a good life, marrying Sarah Exline and raising nine children.

A century later, the Stinchcomb family had moved on and decided to donate the old homestead and the land that had grown from it to the city. It became part of the integral water system known as the Lake Overholser Sedimentation Basin, keeping sediment settling upriver rather than filling up the lake. In 1983, following the Stinchcombs' donation, the parks department decided to make better use of the land around the basins. It couldn't be built on due to threats of flooding, making it perfect for wildlife protection. The city council then renamed the refuge in honor of Lee Stinchcomb.

Stinchcomb Wildlife Refuge hosts many bird species, from wood ducks to Carolina wrens to red-tailed hawks and white-faced ibises.

Top: *The official entrance to the walking trails on one side of the Stinchcomb Wildlife Refuge.* Bottom: *As the sign says, magic happens here.*

Today, the park offers a five-mile walking and biking trail on its east side, accessed from a small parking lot near Bethany High School. The west side is more rugged but offers charming views from North County Line Road. The park is split in half by the river, so the best way to enjoy the park is by boat, usually by coming up under the Northwest 39th Expressway bridge. Whether in a canoe or kayak, the peaceful river and four basins give perfect opportunities for fishing, bird-watching, or simply taking in the sights of a marsh forest in the midst of OKC.

THE GENUINE POPULIST

Who was Oklahoma's blind senator?

There are few people more dedicated through their lifetimes than Senator Thomas Gore. Born in Mississippi in 1870, he was struck blind by the age of 20 after two different accidents. Undeterred, Gore focused on his skills in oratory and studied law. From there, he joined the Populist movement of William Jennings Bryan, and like Bryan, he would ultimately become a Progressive Democrat as national politics shifted around him.

Gore was famous for his modesty and distrust of big politics: "I would rather be a humble private in the ranks of those who struggle for justice and equality than to be a minion of plutocracy, though adorned with purple and gold." Upon its statehood, Oklahoma elected Gore to be one of its two first senators and overwhelmingly reelected him in 1909. In 1914, dirty politicians tried to frame him with a prostitution trap by inviting him to a woman's hotel room, but a scandal refused to form. No one would believe it.

A staunch isolationist until the declaration of war that brought the United States into World War I, Gore failed to be renominated to the Senate in 1921. He came back to the Senate again in 1931 as a fiscally conservative voice opposing national welfare while promoting local relief from the Great Depression. His voice of individualism, the same as it had always had been,

---

Senator Gore stood as the sole vote against the Works Progress Administration (WPA), suspecting it would be used to "dole spoils." He said, "I cannot consent to buy votes with the people's money."

Top: *Senator Gore's final resting place in Fairlawn Cemetery.* Inset: *Portrait of Senator Thomas Gore. Photo courtesy of Wikimedia Commons*

THOMAS GORE MEMORIAL

WHAT: Burial place of Oklahoma's blind senator

WHERE: Fairlawn Cemetery, 2700 N Shartel Ave., directly north of the south entrance

COST: Free

PRO TIP: You may have heard of his grandson, Gore Vidal.

again moved out of public favor, leading to his defeat in 1936. Gore continued to practice law until his death in 1949, and he was buried in Oklahoma City.

Gore made it clear how he felt about his state: "I love Oklahoma. I love every blade of her grass. I love every grain of her sands. I am proud of her past, and I am confident of her future. The virtues that made us great in the past can keep us great in the future. We must march, and not merely mark time."

THE OLD INTERURBAN

What happened to Oklahoma City's original streetcars?

Streetcars are running back and forth on streets downtown in Oklahoma City, adding an exciting burst of energy while helping people get around without worries about parking. Everything old is new again, as just a century earlier, people were getting around much the same way on the old Oklahoma Railway Company (ORC) trolleys.

It began in 1901, when city developers such as Anton Classen and John Shartel (both of whom have extensive streets named after them) started the Metropolitan Railway, which merged with the Oklahoma City Railway Company to become the ORC in 1907. Most people were still getting around by horsepower in those days, and the simple option of stepping on an electric streetcar made it easy to get around town.

Other electric rail lines ran outside the city, gaining the nickname "Interurban" because they extended to nearby cities: north to Guthrie, south to Norman, and west through Bethany out to El Reno. Though the tracks are just about gone, there are a few signs the

OKLAHOMA CITY STREETCAR

WHAT: Easy mass transit all year round

WHERE: Stations throughout downtown, from NW 11th St. and Dewey Ave. to east of Bricktown

COST: $1/hr or $3/day pass

PRO TIP: Park at the Arts District, Sheridan Walker, Century Center, or Convention Center garages, and use your parking receipt as a ticket for two to ride free on the streetcar for 24 hours.

In their heyday, streetcars went as far as Lincoln Park and across the river to Stockyards City and Capitol Hill.

Top: *In the Oklahoma Railway Company's heyday, workers pose with their streetcars. Photo courtesy of Metropolitan Library System.* Bottom: *Old is new again, with streetcars running downtown. Photo courtesy of Dennis Spielman*

railway left behind, such as the Interurban restaurants started in the old station in Norman.

Automobiles came in big after World War I, and even more so after World War II. The rail lines attempted to adapt with rubber-tired electric buses, but the gas buses of the Oklahoma Transportation Company bought out the struggling old system. By 1947, the streetcars were gone and broken up for scrap.

Then, in 2009, Oklahoma City voters decided to bring the rails back as part of the Metropolitan Area Projects Plan (MAPS) 3 package. Construction was completed in 2018 on a $135 million investment to get back to where the city was 100 years ago.

NOT-SO-INVISIBLE MAN

What famous writer found his inspiration in Oklahoma City?

"You never can tell," people like to say about the origins of famous people. Ralph Waldo Ellison, one of America's true literary giants, was born in Oklahoma City in 1913. He attended Frederick Douglass High School, graduating a year late because he was doing too many music performances after taking private trumpet lessons from the conductor of the Oklahoma City Orchestra. He shined shoes on Second Street, washed cars on Classen Avenue, and waited tables at the country club in Nichols Hills. He was much like any other young Black man in Oklahoma City, yet there was something special about him that he had to get out.

In 1930, Ellison headed to college at the Tuskegee Institute and then trekked to New York City, where he would make his name as a writer. He returned to Oklahoma City in 1953 upon winning the National Book award for *Invisible Man*, telling reporters, "I thought if I came back home and looked around, the ideas for my next book would take a more definite form." That

RALPH ELLISON LIBRARY

WHAT: Located in OKC's historically Black neighborhood, the library has some of the most foot traffic of any in the city.

WHERE: 2000 NE 23rd St.

COST: Free, with small fees for some services

PRO TIP: Check out clubs for STEAM, creative writing, quilting, and the Urban Poets.

The Ralph Ellison Memorial in New York City is known to be the largest monument to a writer in the city, portraying a cutout image of an invisible man in a bronze plate.

Top: *Portrait of Ralph Waldo Ellison. Photo courtesy of Metropolitan Library System.* Inset: *Ellison's namesake library on Northeast 23rd Street.*

second novel would ultimately become his unfinished *Juneteenth*, with which he struggled the rest of his life.

In 1975, Ellison returned again, this time to dedicate a public library named in his honor on Northeast 23rd Street, a place that would have been far out of range for African Americans in the days of segregation. In Ellison's day, Oklahoma City ordinances prevented anyone of color from living north of Second Street. The vibrant community pushed back, living on the *north* side of Second and building up a neighborhood of businesses that would come to be known as Deep Deuce.

SCHOOL ON THE HILLTOP

What's the oldest school in Oklahoma City?

The day after the Land Run, Oklahoma City had a population of thousands but no roads, utilities, or schools. While construction would take time, it did not take long at all for classes to get going. The Metropolitan Library reports that the first recorded school in OKC was Mrs. L. H. North's subscription school, opened June 1, 1889. Students paid roughly $1.50 each month (with scholarships available and higher costs for higher grade levels) to sit on nail kegs in a tent under a cottonwood tree.

Soon, more schools were organized, and Oklahoma City began its public school system in 1891. For the next few years, classes were paid for by taxes, but classrooms had to be rented out of shops and hotels. The first schoolhouse was the African American Douglass School, founded March 1. When bond money finally became available to the wards for construction, they rushed to build Washington School at 315 South Walker Avenue, which was the first to open

MOUNT ST. MARY CATHOLIC HIGH SCHOOL

WHAT: Historic education going strong in its second century

WHERE: 2801 S Shartel Ave.

COST: Private school tuition, with scholarships available

PRO TIP: For Oklahoma City's Sacred Heart High School, check the church across the street.

For many years, Mount St. Mary's was the tallest building south of the river and was used as a landmark for travelers to get their bearings.

Top: *A historical postcard shows Mount St. Mary's in its early days.* Inset: *Mount St. Mary's stands proud to this very day.*

in 1895. Finished second, Emerson had to be rebuilt in 1911 after a terrible fire. The oldest schoolhouse still going today is actually across the river, Mount Saint Mary's.

In 1901, the Catholic populace of Oklahoma City invited the Sisters of Mercy to start religious education for their daughters. Land was donated near Capitol Hill, and an impressive brick building was built in 1903. To this day, it stands tall and admirable, overlooking the broad plain from its hilltop perch. Some things have changed over the years, such as the addition in 1910 of day-school students, who rode the trolley to classes, and the school becoming coed in 1950. Newly renovated with a $6 million endowment campaign, it looks just as sharp as it did more than 100 years ago.

COLCORD: LAW & BUSINESS

Why is there a building named after Oklahoma City's first police chief?

The neon glow of "Colcord" has been part of the Oklahoma City skyline for years, but the history of the man behind it might surprise those who haven't heard too much about him. Charles Francis Colcord was born on a Kentucky plantation, the son of a Confederate colonel. After the war, the Colcords moved to a ranch near Corpus Christi, Texas, where 12-year-old Charley mastered herding and even participated in a drive up the Chisholm Trail in 1876. He returned to Oklahoma for the Land Run of 1889, claiming near Hennessey. Selling the farm plot within days, Colcord moved to Oklahoma City and soon found himself elected chief of police to try to keep order in the rowdy new town.

Colcord's work with law enforcement expanded when the official government came into being in 1890, and he was promoted to sheriff of Oklahoma County. Never one to stay still, Colcord made a new claim in the Land Run of 1893 and joined the US Marshals, where he caught five members of the Dalton gang and saw them hanged. Then he was back, promoting city development and driving the need for the Oklahoma City stockyards. About as Oklahoman as a man can get, Colcord soon added "oilman" to his repertoire.

COLCORD HOTEL

WHAT: Modern hotel in a historic building

WHERE: 15 N Robinson Ave.

COST: Presidential Suite, $1,200/night

PRO TIP: Park the car for the night and hop on the streetcar across the street for access throughout downtown and Midtown.

Left: *Colcord's building still bears his illuminated signature.* Inset: *The marblework in the Colcord lobby is among the most beautiful in the city.*

Speculating in oil in the early days of Oklahoma paid handsomely, but Colcord knew not to depend on the money being permanent. He invested his speculation profits from the Glenn Pool field into Oklahoma City's first skyscraper, the 12-story Colcord Building, opened in 1910. Originally, it was meant as an office building, but, in 2006, extensive renovations recreated it as a boutique hotel. With Colcord's diverse business interests, he would certainly be proud.

This OKC building isn't the only thing with Colcord's name: the town of Colcord in eastern Oklahoma became his namesake in 1928, changing its name from Little Tulsa.

WILD MARY SUDIK

Who spewed oil from the capitol to the University of Oklahoma in Norman?

Today, Oklahoma City is well-known for its oil companies, but that was not the case until December 4, 1928, when the Oklahoma City Number One oil well struck black gold. With plenty of road access and available workers, the Oklahoma City field blossomed with wells so fast that they were pumping within city limits only 17 months later. It would have been even sooner, but ordinances from the city council and corporation commission tried to contain the spread to a reasonable pace. Fears of what could happen would be realized on March 26, 1930, when a well went wild.

What is today the southeast corner of the intersection of Interstate 240 and South Bryant Avenue was once the Sudik Dairy. The Sudiks were Czech immigrants who had come to Oklahoma simply to farm. Offers of oil royalties sounded like a good side income, so Mrs. Mary Sudik signed the papers to allow drilling on their property. The first well, nicknamed "Mary Sudik #1," ended up doing better than expected, explosively so. Roughnecks drilling into the oil formation neglected signs of building pressure beneath the well, which erupted with natural gas and oil into a geyser that soared hundreds of feet into the air.

Oil went everywhere—48,000 barrels of it each day. The spray was so intensive that black goo rained down on the capitol five miles to the north. Then, the wind changed, and oil was found on

---

The broken valve that turned the Mary Sudik #1 wild may be seen in the oil and gas exhibit at the Oklahoma History Center.

DEVON ENERGY OIL AND GAS PARK

WHAT: Walk through a collection of historical oil rigs to see how times have changed.

WHERE: 800 Nazih Zuhdi Dr.

COST: Free

PRO TIP: Head south across the parking lot to check out the Red River Journey for surprising history about Oklahoma's southern border.

Top: *The view as the Mary Sudik #1 went wild in 1930. Photo courtesy of the Metropolitan Library System.* Bottom: *Historical oil field equipment intrigues visitors at the Oklahoma History Museum.*

roofs as far as the University of Oklahoma campus, 10 miles to the south. Crews tried to alleviate the pressure, but it wasn't until newly developed equipment of double die casing managed to stymie the well with a two-ton cap.

With production finally under control, the Oklahoma City field would become one of the most prominent oil-producing sites anywhere in the nation for the next two decades.

OIL WELLS AT THE STATE CAPITOL

How did those oil wells get there?

Even after Oklahoma City won the hard-fought 1911 campaign to move the state capital south from Guthrie, there was much contention about where to place the capitol building. The state seal (the official stamp for government business, not the marble design on the capitol floor) had been smuggled out of Guthrie in a bundle of laundry, but Oklahoma City had nowhere to house it. Oklahoma government operated out of hotel rooms and Irving High School for nearly a decade before the capitol was ready for business.

As incentive to build the capitol on the northwest side of town, Oklahoma City developers I. M. Putnam and John W. Shartel offered 1,600 acres and $1.7 million cash. They owned all the land around it, meaning they would cinch up development for all time, which made their opponents nervous. Complaining that the 20-minute railway ride from the station was too long, legislators rejected their offer and instead purchased half of the 160-acre lots

CAPITOL SITE NO. 1, AKA PETUNIA

WHAT: A working oil well on capitol grounds

WHERE: 2300 N Lincoln Blvd.

COST: Nope, it *made* money for the state!

PRO TIP: No other state capitol in the nation can boast working oil wells.

Oklahoma is well-known as the only state with oil rigs on its capitol grounds. These aren't decorative; they are actual oil wells!

Top: *Oil wells stand before the Oklahoma State Capitol, something no other capitol can boast.* Inset: *All down Lincoln Boulevard, oil wells once pumped money for the state.*

from land commissioner William Harn and farmer J. J. Culbertson, only a seven-minute ride away. This established the capitol where it is today, northeast of the Deep Deuce district.

The choice proved a lucky one just a few years later, when the Oklahoma City Oil Field was discovered on the east side of town. The new capitol was right on top of the patch, and more than two dozen wells have been opened over the years. The first was drilled straight into a flower garden in 1941 and earned the nickname "Petunia" from the flowers around it. It has drawn up nearly two million barrels of oil over the many years, which was wealth pumped straight into the state treasury.

GUBERNATORIAL GHOST

Who haunts the Oklahoma Governor's Mansion?

The Roaring Twenties were famous for their prosperity, and Oklahoma had a lion's share with the booming oil industry. State government was flush with cash, especially after oil was discovered right under the capitol itself. In 1927, lawmakers decided to spend $100,000 to finally build a governor's mansion on the grassy field east of the legislature, that had been designated for it 13 years earlier. The 14,000-square-foot house opened with 19 rooms (now consolidated to 12) including bedrooms, dining room, library, parlor, and a grand ballroom on the third floor.

Through the years, guests and residents have noted strange occurrences there. Shadows seem to move on their own, floors creak as if someone were walking on them when no one is in that room, and even a deep voice with a heavy accent has been heard. Most famously, people trip on the stairs in the main hall. Whether going up or down, it always seems to be on the same step, the third

OKLAHOMA GOVERNOR'S MANSION TOURS

WHAT: A guided walking tour of the mansion house

WHERE: 820 NE 23rd St.

COST: Free

PRO TIP: Tours are generally available on Wednesdays September through May. Call (405) 528-2020 to confirm.

The most famous sighting of the ghost was by the children of Gov. Frank Keating while watching television in the basement. He stood over their shoulders and watched, too!

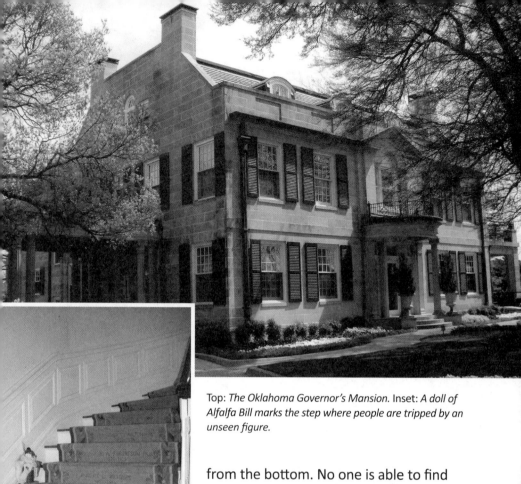

Top: *The Oklahoma Governor's Mansion.* Inset: *A doll of Alfalfa Bill marks the step where people are tripped by an unseen figure.*

from the bottom. No one is able to find what tripped them, and carpenters have even measured the steps without finding anything out of order. The legend goes that it is the ghost of William H. "Alfalfa Bill" Murray, Oklahoma's ninth governor.

Murray was quite a character during his Great Depression term from 1931 to 1935. Elected on a platform of racism and anti-big business, he holds the record for numbers of times calling out the National Guard. He used them to police oil wells to enforce production caps, to control crowds at University of Oklahoma football games, and once to invade Texas over a dispute with the bridge across the Red River. He focused on local relief, including opening the mansion grounds to gardening and harvesting a crop of potatoes, which were processed for storage through the mansion's study windows.

FILM ROW

Why do their basements have six-inch steel doors?

Moviegoing has changed over the years, but not nearly as much as movie distribution. In the early days, reels of silver nitrate film had to be delivered by hand to movie houses. They were extremely volatile, and a single spark could make the film explode. Instead of carting dangerous reels all over the country, movie studios set up regional "film exchanges" where they would deliver the film and bring in local managers to see what movies they wanted to show. For two quarters, cinema managers could settle into screening rooms and watch an unreleased film.

In the 1920s, Oklahoma City served as the film exchange for the state, as well as parts of Texas and Arkansas. To this day, buildings in the Film Row district are marked with the studio logos of Paramount, MGM, and Fox. Due to film fires, the buildings were mandated to be built with

RODEO CINEMA ON FILM ROW

WHAT: Movies in an original Paramount screening room

WHERE: 701 W Sheridan Ave.

COST: Tickets usually run $7.50 to $9.50.

PRO TIP: During the film, sneak a look at the windows to the projector room—the ghost of the former projectionist is said to still be at work!

Oklahoma served as the base for filmmaker Arthur Ramsey (son of W. R. Ramsey), who pioneered making newsreels with coverage of the Dust Bowl and Governor Murray's Toll Bridge War.

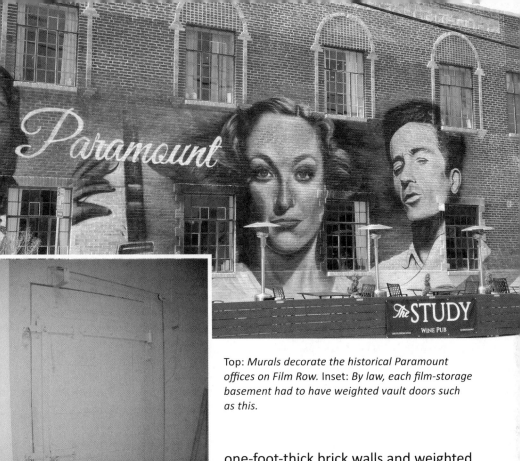

Top: *Murals decorate the historical Paramount offices on Film Row.* Inset: *By law, each film-storage basement had to have weighted vault doors such as this.*

one-foot-thick brick walls and weighted vault doors on their basement storage. Even with careful handling, there were two cases of fires, in 1929 and 1933, that destroyed thousands of reels of film. The costly explosions could have been even worse, but thankfully they were contained inside the sturdy buildings.

When film became more stable, the old exchanges died out, but Oklahoma City's row of studio offices miraculously remained. It was a rundown neighborhood and largely ignored so near downtown, but rediscovery in the early 2000s led to renewal. Today, Film Row is packed with restaurants, boutique shops, outdoor music, and theater-going experiences, both in cinema and Carpenter Square Theatre on the north side. Iconic building façades match modern sidewalks, colored to look like stars and strips of film.

SPEAKEASY LEGENDS

Where was *the* hangout for gamblers and gangsters during Prohibition?

There is a fascinating and shadowy history about the longtime hangout tucked into the forested hills north of the city. How far back it goes is a bit of a mystery, but by the 1920s, there was clearly a nightclub going strong at 1226 Northeast 63rd Street. At the time, it was so far into the countryside that newspaper ads gave directions instead of an address: curious customers could go three blocks north of the capitol and then east four blocks. Many people say the ads kept up the façade of the restaurant, which served as a cover for the gambling hall and speakeasy down below.

The site went through many names, including the English Tavern and Mitchell's Oak Cliff Night Club. It was remodeled with a horse-racing theme as the Kentucky Club in 1938, but most folks know it historically as County Line BBQ, which closed in 2010. The building didn't remain empty long; it became the new home of Gabriella's in 2012.

Gangster Pretty Boy Floyd frequented the club, often rubbing elbows with Oklahoma state lawmakers out for a night of revelry.

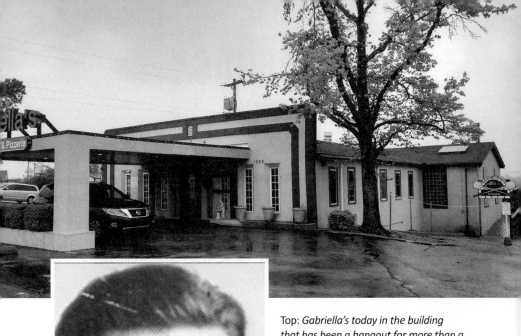

Top: *Gabriella's today in the building that has been a hangout for more than a century.* Inset: *Pretty Boy Floyd was known to hang out here in its speakeasy days.* Photo courtesy of Wikimedia Commons

Rumors about the old place run wild, including the story of a dapper ghost named Russell, who was shot in a fit of passion next to the fireplace near the bar. Tales are told of the club being a haven for liquor and gambling, including tables that could rotate into walls and hidey-holes in the floor to stash whiskey and money at a moment's notice in case of a police raid. It was supposed to have been supplied by stills kept hidden nearby in the trees. John W. Bell, who served as chef at the Kentucky Club for more than three decades, called the legends "a bunch of malarkey." However, a fire in 1949 destroyed the original building. Perhaps it took the sneaky architecture of the heyday speakeasy with it.

SKIRVIN'S LEGACY

What's the true story behind the Skirvin?

W. B. "Bill" Skirvin came to Oklahoma City in 1906. He'd been in Oklahoma before, making the Land Run in Guthrie before selling out to move to Galveston, Texas. After the Hurricane of 1900, his fortunes were troubled, and Skirvin hoped he'd be able to make it rich again in the booming Oklahoma frontier. With early investments in oil, he did very well, indeed.

Skirvin put his money to work, investing in buying up downtown lots that he would turn into the destination hotel for Oklahoma City. When it opened to the fanfare of thousands, it was two towers with 10 stories. By 1930, it had expanded to add another tower to the east and three more floors on top. Skirvin conducted business out of the hotel lobby, which was famously the only hotel in the city to have tile flooring instead of carpet so that he could eat peanuts and have staff sweep up the shells without a problem.

Plenty of wild stories have emerged from over the decades. During Prohibition (which started in 1907 in Oklahoma as part of

> ### THE SKIRVIN HILTON
>
> **WHAT:** Oklahoma City's most charming hotel
>
> **WHERE:** 1 Park Ave.
>
> **COST:** Check the hotel website for room rates and specials.
>
> **PRO TIP:** Treat yourself to a presidential suite on the 10th floor.

The Skirvin Hotel has served the rich and famous for decades, hosting presidents, dignitaries, and stars, including Gloria Swanson, Bob Hope, Frank Sinatra, and Elvis Presley.

Top: *A haunting view of the Skirvin Hotel.* Inset: *The Hilton remodel revealed beautiful tiles in the original Skirvin lobby.*

statehood), the 10th floor of the Skirvin was the place to get a drink. Whenever police raided it, they had to run up 10 flights of stairs, during which time the front desk would call up the guests and suggest, if there was anything they didn't want the police to find, they should pour it out the window. After the oil crash of 1986, the Skirvin closed up and became a legendary haunt until it was remodeled and reopened by Hilton in 2007. People say it's so luxurious that numerous guests continue to dwell there as ghosts, including Mr. Skirvin himself, his daughter, Ambassador Perle Mesta, and a young lady called Effie who chases NBA players.

STRANGE NIGHTS AT BELLE ISLE

Why were people spooked at one of OKC's earliest parks?

With Oklahoma City growing by leaps and bounds, the Oklahoma Railway Company made getting around easy with electric streetcars. All that electricity needed to come from somewhere, so an enormous power plant was built on the north side of town near the end of the old route, along today's Classen Boulevard. With ridership down after work on evenings and weekends, Anton Classen came up with a plan to use that extra electricity to get people out and about to the well-lit grounds of a park around the power plant. He called it Belle Isle. This replaced Delmar Gardens as the spot for relaxation in Oklahoma City's second chapter.

At midnight on May 3, 1924, something strange appeared in the sky over the heads of hundreds of people visiting the park. *The Oklahoman* reported it hung over Belle Isle at about 1,000 feet for nearly half an hour before heading northwest. It then rose to 1,400 feet and continued north to Britton Road. Whatever it was hung too long in the sky to be a shooting star, and it was too still to be an airplane. Some speculated it was a lantern on a balloon, but no balloon could ever be spotted carrying the strange light.

Unidentified flying objects are one thing, but Belle Isle later became known as a haunted place. A larger power plant was

---

Though the lake was filled in and the park built over, Belle Isle still lives on in memory through its name shared with a library, shopping district, and neighborhood.

ic Island, Belle Isle,
clahoma City, Okla.

Top: *A postcard shows the relaxing times to be had at Belle Isle. Courtesy of the Metropolitan Library System.* Inset: *An aerial view of the power station and lake at Belle Isle. Photo courtesy of the Metropolitan Library System.*

BELLE ISLE RESTAURANT & BREWERY

WHAT: Tasty eats and live music in the spirit of Belle Isle

WHERE: 1900 Northwest Expy., #44R

COST: Grab a burger or a pizza for around $10.

PRO TIP: Check out their events webpage for upcoming shows. No word on UFOs or ghosts yet.

built there in 1930, which ran until 1980 through Oklahoma Gas & Electric (OG&E). Afterward, it became the stuff of legend, with a ghostly girl said to appear in the third-story windows, even though the old floor had collapsed years before. The plant was demolished in 1999 after a teen fell to her death exploring the ruin for her own ghostly encounter.

DINNER AT O. A.'S

Would you rather dine at a mayor's house or a buffalo ranch? Why not both?

The northeast side of Oklahoma City remained rural for decades while things developed to the west. Even today, it is easy to go past Interstate 35 and onto roads surrounded by fields with horses and cattle within a few miles. In the earlier days of Oklahoma City, where now Interstate 35 and US Route 66 cross paths, there once was a wide-open ranch cut out among the blackjack oaks where the buffalo roamed. Former Oklahoma City mayor Otto "O. A." Cargill recaptured a bit of the Wild West by raising up a herd of American bison, then an endangered species from rampant hunting in the 19th century.

Cargill had worked his way up from being a streetcar conductor through the police force to defense attorney and finally mayor in 1923. He stood six foot six inches tall and, as *The Oklahoman* described, "dominated a courtroom." Like many Oklahoma politicians of

PETROLEUM CLUB NORTH

WHAT: Decadent dining at the club's Edmond location

WHERE: 1 N Sooner Rd., Edmond, OK

COST: It's impolite to discuss money at the table.

PRO TIP: An entire room has been dedicated to the wine collection, making it one of the most complete in Oklahoma.

Cargill ran his buffalo herd when the American Bison Society estimated only a few thousand buffalo were still living, out of the tens of millions that once ruled the Great Plains.

Left: *Mayor Cargill's official portrait.* Inset: *Buffalo roam at Cargill's ranch in this historical postcard. Photos courtesy of the Metropolitan Library System*

the era, Cargill faced his own legal issues, such as the lynching of Claude Chandler in an out-of-jurisdiction moonshine raid while Cargill was district attorney of Oklahoma County. Perjury convictions haunted him later in life, when Oklahoma Supreme Court bribery scandals broke out in the 1960s. He retired to his 4,000-square-foot ranch home, where he spent his days watching the buffalo.

After Cargill passed, the home was sold in 1985 to become the Greystone Restaurant, and today it is the northernmost dining room of the prestigious Petroleum Club. The house remained intact while architects added 6,000 square feet and a grand entrance. As something of a relic, the stone fireplace is made from the transplanted stones of the Missouri log cabin where Cargill was born in 1885.

RIDING THE RAILS

Where can you sit back and watch the landscape go by?

Before the Interstate Highway System and airplanes became fashionable, folks needed to hop a train to get anywhere farther than a horse could take them. Railroads laid the groundwork for Oklahoma, having been in the Unassigned Lands years before most settlers even arrived. Towns such as Guthrie, Norman, and Oklahoma City exist because there were train stations there already. In fact, for its first few years, this town was known as "Oklahoma Station" before "city" was officially added. While much of train travel is bygone when people can just drive a car, there is still southbound travel service that carries tens of thousands of passengers every year.

The Heartland Flyer began service in 1999, making daily runs to Fort Worth, Texas. Today, Oklahomans can travel by rail, changing to other trains that take them as far as Seattle, Washington; Miami, Florida; or Brunswick, Maine. While not as fast as plane travel, it proves to be much less stressful, often less costly, and far more scenic as the American landscape rolls by.

A trip from Oklahoma City begins at the platform above the Santa Fe Railway depot, listed on the National Register of Historic Places in 2015. The depot itself is the office for OKC transit services, but it still shows the grandeur of Jazz Age travel. Opened in 1934 and renovated in 2017, the depot glows, with aluminum and creamy limestone still showcasing the chandelier's geometric

HEARTLAND FLYER

WHAT: Daily connections from Oklahoma City to Fort Worth

WHERE: 100 S E.K. Gaylord Blvd.

COST: $31 one-way

PRO TIP: The train also makes stops in Norman, Purcell, Pauls Valley, Ardmore, and Gainesville, FL, making it perfect for a day trip.

Left: *The interior of the Santa Fe station glows with art deco majesty.* Inset: *Train travelers today come to Oklahoma City in the same spot as they did when it was Oklahoma Station, though some things have changed.*

patterns that were iconic of the era. Trains head south in the morning and come back from Texas in the afternoon, arriving a little after 9 p.m. With Amtrak accepting bicycles, it makes for a perfect way to get around without a car and explore, as travelers did years ago.

Today's depot is the third for Oklahoma City, all built on the same site: first a wooden one, then brick with an iconic tower, and finally the glamorous limestone one.

FATHER OF
THE ELECTRIC GUITAR

How did Charlie Christian change American music forever?

Everything in Charlie Christian's life seems to have been sped up. Charles Henry Christian moved to Oklahoma City when he was two years old and, by age 10, he had mastered the trumpet. At 12 he turned to the guitar; he soon made his own out of cigar boxes. Before graduating Douglass High School, Christian was playing up and down Deep Deuce with Jazz greats Eddie Durham and Jim Daddy Walker at venues such as Slaughter's Hall.

In 1937, everything changed when Christian came across a new, technologically advanced musical device: the electric guitar. He tinkered with the instrument, even designing his own to play a unique style. Borrowing from his experience with brass, Christian developed his "single-string technique," which helped draw the guitar out from a supporting role in the rhythm section to the stage-center solo instrument known today.

Music promoter John Hammond picked up Christian, who soon joined Big Band icon Benny Goodman. Christian was creating music so new that Goodman didn't understand he needed to plug in an amplifier during his audition; it wasn't until Hammond sneaked Christian onto stage that Goodman heard what he could do. Christian then played with the Goodman Sextet and the full orchestra. When not on tour, Christian played in clubs in Harlem, especially Minton's, where he played with Dizzy Gillespie, Charlie

---

Slaughter's Hall was a project of Dr. W. H. Slaughter, the first Black doctor in Oklahoma City, to bring music to the community. Without it, we wouldn't have the music we do today.

Bottom right: *Portrait of Charlie Christian at the Waldorf Astoria in 1939. Courtesy of Wikimedia Commons.* Inset: *Slaughter's Hall as it looked in Charlie Christian's day. Photo courtesy of the Metropolitan Library System*

laughter Bldg, or Doctors' Row , Okla. City, Okla.

Parker, and Thelonious Monk. Their jam sessions would evolve into bebop as a new musical era, largely in part to Christian's guitar work.

In 1941, Charlie Christian developed rasping coughs, indicating tuberculosis. He checked into Staten Island's Seaview Sanatorium, where he died on March 2, 1942, at only 24 years old. Already, Christian had made an impact on the world of music that can still be heard today.

DR. HAYWOOD'S BUILDING

Where can you grab a bite to eat in an old doctor's office?

In 1908, surgeon William L. Haywood was on a train from Indiana to California when he began to feel ill. He disembarked at Guthrie, Oklahoma, but soon found he had to travel on to Oklahoma City to find a Black doctor, due to segregated medicine. Dr. W. H. Slaughter treated him and, as they spoke, Slaughter suggested that Haywood stay in Oklahoma City. Orphaned at five years old, Haywood had worked hard to become a doctor, and here was a place of hardworking folks, just like himself, in the brand-new town.

The Land Run that settled Oklahoma City wasn't just whites, and a Black community called Sandtown grew up on the eastern side of the Wholesale District along the river. By 1910, Oklahoma City had an African American population of 6,700, growing northward to Second Street and beyond. Haywood decided to join the community and found his place as doctor and longtime director of the choir at Avery Chapel AME Church.

DEEP DEUCE GRILL

WHAT: Modern bar and grill in a classic building

WHERE: 307 NE 2nd St.

COST: An awesome meal for about $12

PRO TIP: Save room for a cookie sundae!

Today known as Deep Deuce, it was called "Deep Second" then. The neighborhood grew up along Second Street, the farthest north people of color were allowed to live until courts overturned city ordinances.

The Deep Deuce Grill now occupies the building that has welcomed customers for a century.

In 1938, Haywood purchased the building at Northeast Second Street, which had been built by developer and confectioner Andrew Rushing, father of blues musician Jimmy "Five by Five" Rushing. Renovating the building, Haywood established a pharmacy downstairs and his offices upstairs. He'd been busy in the meantime, founding the Utopia Hospital in 1921, often referred to as the first African American hospital west of the Mississippi River. Haywood also helped Dr. Slaughter to found the Great Western Hospital and served as chief of staff and then director at the Oklahoma University Hospital, overseeing integration in enrollment, teaching, placement, and cafeteria services.

THE INVENTION OF THE SHOPPING CART

How did Oklahoma figure into one of the world's most-used inventions?

In 1937, Oklahoma City grocer Sylvan Goldman had a problem. He had been very successful in the grocery business since he and his brother had opened Goldman Brothers Wholesale Fruits and Produce in 1919. Different ventures through his career had taken him from the heights of owning the Sun Grocery Company, the first chain of supermarkets in Oklahoma, to losing a fortune in the stock market crash in 1929. With a new chain of Humpty Dumpty supermarkets in Oklahoma City, Goldman was struggling, along with many in the Great Depression. People still needed to eat, but they would only buy as much as they could carry, even though food storage like canning and iceboxes had drastically increased shelf life. Suddenly Goldman had the idea to boost sales by getting people to carry more.

Working with store engineer Frank Young, Goldman ironed out the idea of a collapsible basket on wheels that would become

SCIENCE MUSEUM OKLAHOMA

WHAT: Hands-on learning about science and engineering

WHERE: 2020 Remington Pl.

COST: $17 for adults, $14 for kids

PRO TIP: Check out the Sylvan Goldman statue upstairs!

Goldman had a famous quote about the grocery business: "The wonderful thing about food is that everyone uses it, and they only use it once."

Left: *The statue of Goldman and his shopping cart at the Science Museum.* Right: *Examples of Goldman's carts in the Hinton Historical Museum. Courtesy of Dennis Spielman.*

today's shopping cart. He tested it at his store in southwest Oklahoma City. At first, it was a flop. Men felt insulted at the suggestion they needed help with their groceries. Women thought it looked too much like a baby buggy.

Goldman turned the idea around by hiring models to walk through the stores, pretending to shop while they used carts. The good-looking folks turned heads, and soon everyone was using carts themselves. Because it was so easy to load the carts with plenty of food, sales went up, just as Goldman had suspected.

A decade later, Orla Watson invented telescoping grocery carts to save even more space at the front of stores and was awarded a patent over Goldman's challenges. Though Goldman lost out and had to pay royalties for the next generation of grocery tech, he had already become a millionaire on cart sales.

THE OKC KIDNAPPING THAT MADE THE FBI

Whom did Machine Gun Kelly kidnap?

It was a quiet Saturday on July 22, 1933, when the bridge game between oilman Charles F. Urschel, his friend Walter Jarrett, and their wives was interrupted by men wielding machine guns. George Kelly and Albert L. Bates forced their way through the door, held the party at gunpoint, and took away Urschel and Jarrett in the back of Kelly's car. After checking the men's wallets to find out which was Urschel, the kidnappers dropped Jarrett off about 10 miles outside of town and took Urschel on to their hideout at Kelly's in-laws' farm in Paradise, Texas.

Kidnapping was a new step for gangsters accustomed to bootlegging and bank robbing, but initially it worked well. They asked for $200,000 ransom, which Urschel's family paid readily enough. Urschel had been Tom Slick's partner in the Cushing oil rush and later married his widow, which combined them into one of the richest families in the state. After the money was delivered, Urschel was let go on July 30. Unfortunately for the kidnappers, that was just the beginning, not the end.

J. Edgar Hoover, director of the Bureau of Investigation, was hungry for a win. His agents weren't allowed to carry weapons and often were confused with Prohibition enforcement officers.

FBI OKLAHOMA CITY CITIZENS ACADEMY ALUMNI ASSOCIATION

WHAT: Partners with law enforcement for outreach and education

WHERE: Discussion groups online and at the Oklahoma City Memorial Museum

COST: $75 dues per year

PRO TIP: Keep an ear out for special training sessions.

Top: *The historical home where the kidnapping went down.* Inset: *Lawmen walk Kelly to trial after his capture.* Photo courtesy of Wikimedia Commons

With kidnappings in the news after the Lindbergh baby, he invested his best agents and their new scientific crime laboratory to catch Kelly. Urschel was a great help, having taken note of turns the car made while he was blindfolded and at what times planes passed overhead. Agents raided the farmhouse, confirmed Urschel's fingerprints there, and tracked Kelly to Tennessee, all within two months. A few weeks later, Kelly was sent to jail for the rest of his life, and Hoover played the media, including claiming Kelly gave up, shouting, "Don't shoot, G-men!" With much commendation, the FBI became its own institution in the Department of Justice less than two years later.

After Urschel, oilmen were so nervous about being kidnapped that they often slipped out of their offices in disguise and, in Tulsa, built networks of tunnels to sneak out of other buildings.

THE PARK-O-METER

What great scourge was invented in Oklahoma?

In 1932, newspaperman Carl Magee had a vision to combat the growing problem of automobiles in Oklahoma City. Over the past two decades, the number of cars in the state had grown from 3,000 to more than 500,000, most of which were in Oklahoma County. The roads were congested enough with drivers, but the real question was where to put them all when it came time to park. Retail customers trying to get to stores found all the good spots downtown locked up by staff, who parked at the beginning of the workday and left their cars to sit until time to head home. Efforts of police to chalk tires were too varied to be successful, because people could be wrongfully ticketed after moving to a new location.

As the head of the Traffic Committee for the city, Magee's dream was simple: charge people to park based on how long they were going to be there. He envisioned a wind-up machine that would take money and count down the time allowed to park. His own patent application for a rough device was made in 1932, and a contest for an improved model was launched by the Engineering Department at Oklahoma State University the next year. Finally, efforts produced a prototype nicknamed the Black Maria that could be readily reproduced by the MacNick Company in Tulsa, well-known for its timing devices for nitroglycerin explosives.

According to the Oklahoma History Center, Magee had been arrested for manslaughter after shooting at a judge in Las Vegas, but he was later acquitted.

Top: *Examples of historical parking meters, with Magee's Park-o-Meter on the far left. Photo courtesy of the Harris & Ewing Collection, Library of Congress.* Inset: *A parking meter today on the site where the first one was installed, almost 90 years ago.*

On July 16, 1935, the Park-O-Meter No. 1 was installed along with 174 of its siblings in downtown Oklahoma City. People spoke out against them, but the devices did work to clean up parking problems, as well as raise money for the city. Soon, parking meters would spread like a plague across the United States.

SITE OF THE FIRST PARKING METER

WHAT: Nearly a century later, there are still parking meters in downtown Oklahoma City.

WHERE: Southeast corner of Park Ave. and Robinson Ave.

COST: 50 cents for 15 minutes or $2 for two hours

NOTABLE: Street parking is free after 6 p.m. and on weekends.

NEIGHBORHOOD OF FIRSTS

Where was the first Mexican restaurant in Oklahoma?

Take a turn toward the north from 23rd Street, between Walker and Lee avenues, and you'll end up in a neighborhood that seems straight out of Santa Fe, New Mexico. That surprising experience was entirely the point when it was first laid out by Oklahoma City developer and dentist Gilbert A. Nichols. He had built homes in Heritage Hills, Mesta Park, Crown Heights, and, of course, Nichols Hills. In 1928, he turned to commercial work with the first shopping district north of downtown, a major shift since the city had largely grown west along the streetcar lines. To keep the area unique, it was all designed in Spanish Revival architecture and called the Spanish Village. The next year, Oklahoma City would dub him the town's "Most Useful Citizen."

Since the 1980s, the neighborhood has been living a renaissance as the Paseo (Spanish for "walk"). Entire blocks are listed on the National Register of Historic Places, with the vast majority of the structures nearing their 100th birthdays.

PASEO ARTS DISTRICT FIRST FRIDAYS

WHAT: Monthly neighborhood shindig with more than 80 artists on the first Friday, 6–9 p.m.

WHERE: 3024 Paseo St.

COST: Free

PRO TIP: Try street parking in the surrounding neighborhood to beat the rush for spots on Paseo itself.

Art has always been a part of the neighborhood, with resident art gallery and studio The Elms opening in 1920, even before the Paseo was a dream.

Top: *The Spanish Revival architecture still shines along the Paseo.* Inset: *One of the entry markers to the historical Paseo walk.*

Built on that foundation of history, the Paseo is best known as one of the most vibrant arts communities in the state, along with shops and restaurants that draw crowds, especially during First Friday events and the annual arts festival.

Fitting with the Southwest aesthetic, the Paseo was the second home of the first Mexican restaurant in Oklahoma. While the food is more recognizable as Tex-Mex rather than traditional Mexican, El Charro gave OKC its first servings of dishes widely recognized today as burritos and tacos. These were rare fare in 1937 when El Charro opened, and it moved to the Paseo as El Charrito after a fire in 1946.

OLDER THAN OKC

Where did the oldest church in Oklahoma City come from?

Trying to determine the oldest church in Oklahoma City presents a complicated question. Counting a church as its people means that several congregations are tied, since the city began all at once with the Land Run. St. Joseph Old Cathedral, First Presbyterian Church, and First United Methodist Church all date back to 1889, although First Presbyterian notes that its services came earliest on April 28, the Sunday after the Land Run.

Counting the oldest church building is another issue altogether. Wooden churches soon went up as Oklahoma City transformed from a collection of tents into an actual town. Those structures have all long passed, and the oldest surviving OKC church building is the brick-and-mortar St. Joseph Old Cathedral. It was built with beams and pews from the original wooden church and was formally dedicated in 1904. The cathedral was damaged in the 1995 bombing and required two years of renovations before being reopened. Though the blast hefted the roof and caused much of the pipe organ to collapse, the crucifix was unscathed and the tabernacle candle still burned.

But the oldest church building in Oklahoma City is actually 60 years older than the first one built in town. Old Trinity of Paseo is a classic, northern Anglican, white-walled church with lattice windows and Gothic beams. It was built in Halifax, Nova Scotia, in 1842, where it served generations of parishioners. After 150 years,

Many of Oklahoma City's oldest churches line up on North Robinson Avenue, creating a small neighborhood that has been dubbed "Church Row."

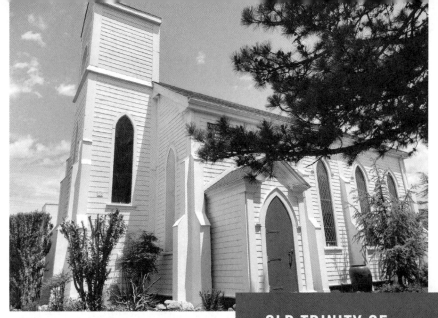

OLD TRINITY OF PASEO EVENT VENUE

WHAT: A rebuilt 1842 Anglican church

WHERE: 3000 N Lee Ave.

COST: Events can run from a few hundred to a few thousand dollars, depending on your glamour.

PRO TIP: Hourly rentals are available, making it a great instructional space.

Top: *Old Trinity church standing in the Paseo today, 80 years older than even the neighborhood.* Bottom: *St. Joseph Old Cathedral in 1956, already well-established in those days. Photo courtesy of the Metropolitan Library System*

it was on the verge of ruin, even as a protected provincial historic site. Photographer Tom Lee brought the surviving pieces of the building including entrances, windows, doors, and jambs, to the Paseo in Oklahoma City, reconstructing the building as an event center in 2001. Today it faces east-west, just as it did 2,000 miles away in Halifax.

OKLAHOMA CITY'S 33-STORY SLIDE

Where can you slide all the way down a skyscraper?

New York City is well-known for its skyscraper competition between the Empire State Building and the Chrysler Building, but not everybody knows that Oklahoma City had its own upward race. The timing was perfect: Oklahoma City was still flush with cash from the oil boom and needed to create jobs for Depression-era workers. The 20-story Dowel Center opened in 1927, but already the plans were being made to beat it with a new, taller building. What building that would be remained the question.

OKC's "Great Race" pitted City Place Tower (then known as Ramsey Tower) against First National Center to see what would become the new crown jewel of the Oklahoma City skyline. Oilman W. R. Ramsey pushed his crew to finish construction first. He'd picked the Starrett Corporation that had built the Empire State Building, so they knew a few things about setting up skyscrapers. The Ramsey Tower was completed in 1931 at 440 feet tall, although First National Center would take the title a few months later with its 446-foot roof and 50-foot spire for good measure.

It wouldn't be until 1971 that the record was beaten by the 36-floor BancFirst Tower, today dwarfed by the 50 floors of the Devon Energy Center. Working at such heights can cause problems during emergencies, but the City Place Tower offered a fast way

HIGH-SPEED SLIDES

WHAT: The tallest dry slide complex in the nation

WHERE: 800 Riversport Dr.

COST: Day passes start at $39.99

PRO TIP: While the 33-story slide is only for emergencies, the 72-foot slides at RIVERSPORT Adventures will take you up to 22 miles per hour.

Bottom: *How the Oklahoma City skyline looked with its newly completed skyscrapers. Photo courtesy of the Metropolitan Library System.* Inset: *City Place Tower today.*

down with a steel slide for its internal fire escape. The slide fits neatly into a closet on each floor, spiraling along a central pole with rounded metal plates. It was lauded in 1931 as a lifesaving innovation. Fortunately, it has never come into emergency use, although local media has taken a trip down with a camera for those curious as to just how dizzyingly long the ride would be!

With its waves of oil money, Oklahoma City has iconic buildings for every architectural era. City Place Tower and First National Center serve as excellent art deco examples.

THE THING ABOUT OUR AIRPORTS

Is it true that Oklahoma City has an airport named after a man who died in a plane crash?

While it's the old joke that folks from Oklahoma City are brave enough to name an airport after a fella who died in a plane crash, that isn't the whole truth. The fact is, we have two airports named after two fellas who died in the same plane crash. Will Rogers World Airport is the bigger one, but local fliers are also familiar with Wiley Post Airport on the northwest side of town, handling business and corporate flights.

Will Rogers is a household name to this day, well-known for his cowboy philosophy and everyman sense of humor. What people today might not remember about him are his careers as a Broadway star with the Ziegfeld Follies, as a widely published author and columnist, and as the highest-paid actor in Hollywood for years in the 1920s and 1930s. Rogers was also an enthusiast for new air technology and became the first jetsetter, traveling to many of his engagements by mail plane.

Wiley Post, meanwhile, was a daring aviator and inventor. He bought his first plane with the payout from losing his eye in an oil rig accident, and soon began winning air races. Along with navigator Harold Gatty, Post set the record of flying around the world in just eight days, 15 hours, and 51 minutes. He then flew around the world by himself and set a new record. In 1934, Post

WILL ROGERS WORLD AIRPORT

WHAT: Flights all over the country (and world)

WHERE: 7100 Terminal Dr.

COST: Flights as low as $47

PRO TIP: Check out the Art at Will installations of Oklahoma-themed sculptures.

Top: *Oklahomans honor air travel advocates with their airport names.*
Bottom: *The last known photo of Rogers and Post, taken during their Alaska trip. Photo courtesy of Wikimedia Commons*

applied his engineering and aerospace knowledge to create a practical pressure suit to fly higher than anyone ever had before.

Their lives ended in 1935. Post invited Rogers on a trip charting a new air route through Alaska, and their experimental plane stalled and crashed outside Point Barrow. Millions mourned the tragedy, a calculated risk by two men who had dedicated themselves to furthering aviation.

Oklahoma City has a third airport, handling experimental craft and ultralights. It's named for Clarence E. Page: World War I pilot, barnstormer, and engineer. (He passed away at home, aged 91.)

FATHER OF THE ELECTRIC GUITAR (page 72)

MANSION ON THE PRAIRIE (p

THE GOLDEN AGE OF RAIL (page 22)

SONIC BOOMS AND SONIC CUPS (page 148)

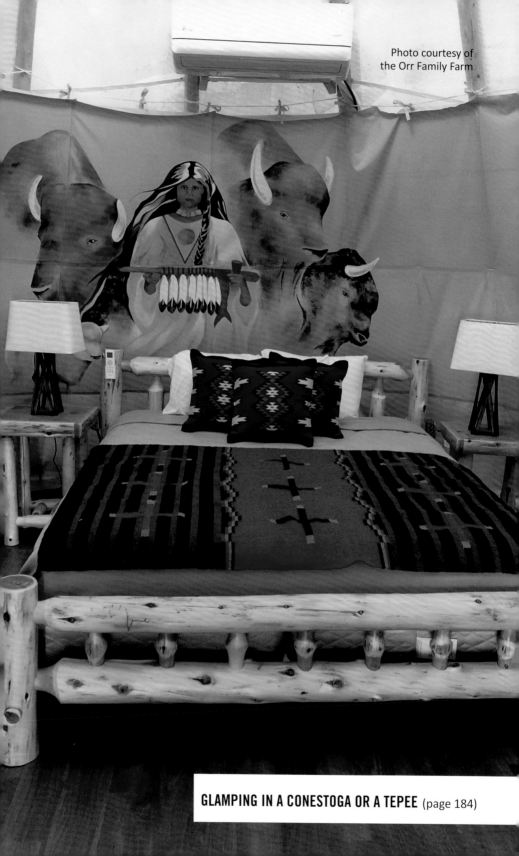

Photo courtesy of the Orr Family Farm

GLAMPING IN A CONESTOGA OR A TEPEE (page 184)

FOUR HUNDRED FEET OF MURALS (page 176)

Photo courtesy of
Dennis Spielman

THE TUNNELS (page 136)

EXOTIC ANIMAL RACING (page 142)

FORGOTTEN DOORS (page 38)

DRESSED UP IN TRUSSES (page 40)

THE BRICKTOWN CANAL'S PREDECESSOR (page 20)

WALK THROUGH THE EXPERIENCE (page 186)

OSLER BUILDING (page 156)

MORE THAN JUST RATTLERS (page 170)

ROSES UNDER GLASS

What's there to do in a garden?

As naturalist John Muir said, "Everybody needs beauty as well as bread, places to play in and pray in, where nature may heal and give strength to body and soul." Oklahoma Citians knew that from the beginning, so in 1912, city leaders bought a dairy farm on the outskirts of town to serve as an extensive park for the growing populace. It was part of W. H. Dunn's 1910 plan that created the Grand Boulevard Loop to surround town with a meandering drive that circled like a crown with four park jewels: Trosper, Lincoln, Woodson, and Will Rogers. Today Will Rogers Gardens serves as one of the best places to hang out with nature, with 30 peaceful acres right in the middle of the city.

Much of the Will Rogers Gardens was created thanks to relief efforts during the Great Depression. Oklahoma was hit hard with the Dust Bowl and struggling oil prices, so it won many of

WILL ROGERS GARDENS HORTICULTURAL CENTER

WHAT: Educational programs and rentals

WHERE: 3400 NW 36th St.

COST: Rent the Exhibition Center for $25/hr. or the Ed Lycan Conservatory for $100/hr.

PRO TIP: Try the hands-on gardening and horticultural classes.

The Margaret Annis Boys Arboretum within Will Rogers Gardens shows hundreds of examples of trees, some originals planted by Henry Walter nearly a century ago.

Top: *The conservatory at the gardens has warmed plants and guests alike for decades.* Inset: *The lake at Will Rogers Gardens.*

the Works Progress Administration (WPA) and Civilian Conservation Corps (CCC) projects that can still be seen today. Beautification at Will Rogers Park (then known as Northwest Park, renamed in 1936 after Rogers perished in a crash) gave the city the extensive ponds, stone plant beds, and scenic overlooks. It has also become home to the Ed Lycan Conservatory, an extensive greenhouse that had first been in Douglass Park and now serves as one of the state's largest collections of succulents and cacti.

Will Rogers Gardens is a busy place, with meetings in the Exhibition Center Hall, shows in the amphitheater, and horticultural workshops, particularly with roses in the Charles E. Sparks Color Garden. People frequently use the gardens as backdrops for wedding photos and the conservatory for ceremonies. Even with all the buzz, its acres among the trees remain a quiet place for a break from urban life.

HALL-OF-FAMERS

What does it take to be in the hall of fame?

Not enough folks have heard of Anna B. Korn. Much of her biography shows a life spent like most of her days. Born in 1869 in Missouri, she moved to El Reno with her husband in 1891. She provided for her family, and she wrote nonfiction and poetry, along with contributing to local clubs. Through these clubs, she served as a booster for the state, authoring the legislation for statehood day and, in 1927, organizing an Oklahoma Hall of Fame that lives on with more than 700 members. Her achievements, along with many of those in the Hall of Fame, show that there are no limits to what is possible for everyone.

If you're wondering who can be in the Oklahoma Hall of Fame, the answer is . . . anyone from Oklahoma! All it takes is to be nominated and approved by the selection committee. The only requirements are that the person must have lived in Oklahoma, performed an outstanding service, and brought honor to the state. Typically,

GAYLORD-PICKENS MUSEUM

WHAT: Interactive exhibits showcasing Oklahoma's Hall of Fame

WHERE: 1400 Classen Dr.

COST: $7 for adults, $5 for students and seniors

PRO TIP: Check out oklahomahof.com for special coupons!

The Mid-Continent Life Building was built by R. T. Stuart, who was inducted into the Hall of Fame in 1957. Stuart and his family lived in an upstairs apartment of the insurance building.

The Oklahoma Hall of Fame is housed in the Gaylord-Pickens Museum, once the glamorous offices of Mid-Continent Life Insurance.

six to eight people each year are added to the roll, showing a wide range of Oklahomans. The list includes astronaut Leroy Gordon Cooper, ambassador Perle Skirvin Mesta, lawman and oilman Charles Colcord, rancher Jim Shoulders, musician Charlie Christian, civic leader Clara Luper, and so many more. Even Mrs. Korn herself was made a member in 1933.

Today, the Oklahoma Hall of Fame is housed in the Gaylord-Pickens Museum, along with interactive exhibits and digital displays. Repurposing the Mid-Continent Life Building while maintaining its original marble and wood paneling, the museum ties together the old and the new with inspiration toward the future.

HOME OF THE THUNDERBIRDS

Who were the soldiers bold enough to be called "thunderbirds"?

What began as an officers' club in 1937 has become one of the most impressive collections of military history anywhere in the nation. In 1974, the Lincoln Park Armory was transformed to house the growing collection of weapons, personal effects, and memorabilia from soldiers who served with the 45th Infantry Division made up of the Oklahoma, Colorado, Arizona, and New Mexico National Guards. Known as the Thunderbirds for the patch bearing the icon of the legendary Native American creature, the division served in World War II's invasion of Sicily, brutal Italian Campaign, and Operation Dragoon, as well as three years of intensive fighting in Korea.

The brothers in arms will never be forgotten, especially with the museum's extensive showcases with the physical memorials to their service to the 45th Infantry Division Association. Visitors will marvel at decades of military action, including relics from the liberation of Dachau and Adolf Hitler's bunker after the capture of Berlin. The Reaves Military Weapons Collection gives examples of firearms from the Revolutionary War to Vietnam, supplemented by personal donations of numerous other weapons. Outside, a 15-acre park displays aircraft, tanks, and unique vehicles from several eras of warfare.

The 45th Infantry Division was organized in 1923 and served until 1968. Its famous Thunderbird insignia was designed by Kiowa artist Woody Big Bow.

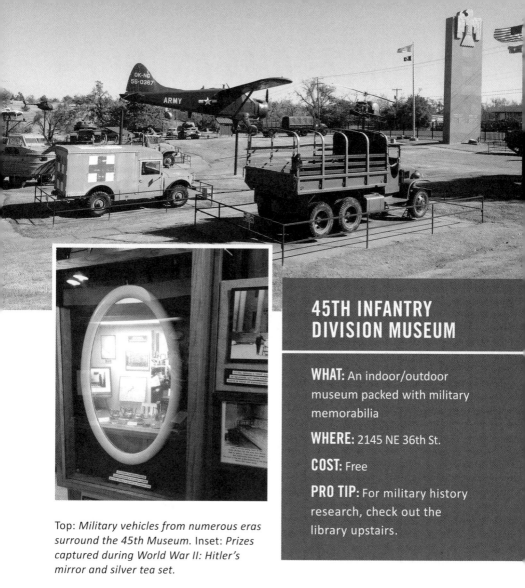

45TH INFANTRY DIVISION MUSEUM

WHAT: An indoor/outdoor museum packed with military memorabilia

WHERE: 2145 NE 36th St.

COST: Free

PRO TIP: For military history research, check out the library upstairs.

Top: *Military vehicles from numerous eras surround the 45th Museum.* Inset: *Prizes captured during World War II: Hitler's mirror and silver tea set.*

The 45th Museum also hosts the Bill Mauldin Cartoon Collection, featuring more than 200 original works by the soldier-turned-Pulitzer-Prize-winning journalist who captured the experience of the front line in his cartoons. Everymen Willie and Joe swapped one-liners to make light of the terrible conditions of war, bringing smiles of understanding to countless thousands of soldiers. Following the war, Mauldin went on to critique civilian life and won a second Pulitzer for his depiction of the weeping Lincoln Memorial after the Kennedy assassination. Mauldin's art and fame all began in 1940 with his first cartoons in the *45th Division News*.

USS *OKLAHOMA* ANCHOR

What's a battleship anchor doing on Broadway?

Leading up to World War II, the USS *Oklahoma* was one of the stars of Battleship Row. She entered service escorting Allied troops across the Atlantic in World War I and ferried President Woodrow Wilson's convoy to sign the Treaty of Paris. Her coming decades of service were humanitarian, including evacuating refugees from the Spanish Civil War, which made her the first American battleship to have a baby born onboard. With war anticipated in the Pacific, the *Oklahoma* was brought together with seven other battleships at Pearl Harbor to make ready defense. They would take the most damage during the attack on December 7, 1941.

OKLAHOMA HISTORY CENTER

WHAT: More than 200,000 square feet of Oklahoma's historical artifacts

WHERE: 800 Nazih Zuhdi Dr.

COST: $10 for adults, $5 for students and seniors

PRO TIP: Keep an eye out for additional USS *Oklahoma* artifacts, including the aft wheel and ship's flag.

More than one in five of the 2,406 people killed in the attack were from the *Oklahoma*. She took nine torpedoes and sank into the harbor. Amid the tragedy, there were many heroes,

Campbell Park has its own ties to OKC history: it was made into greenspace after widening Broadway Avenue, originally a raised field that was later leveled by the WPA.

Left: *Another relic of the USS* Oklahoma *is its formal punchbowl, which is kept at the Governor's Mansion.* Inset: *An anchor of the USS* Oklahoma *stands vigilant on Broadway Avenue.*

and three *Oklahoma* sailors were awarded the Medal of Honor for their actions.

The *Oklahoma's* story did not end there, as the Navy attempted to tow her remains back for repairs. The damage proved too deep, however, and the *Oklahoma* sank en route to San Francisco. Parts have been rescued, including one 10-ton anchor that was brought as a monument to *Oklahoma's* namesake state through efforts of men such as Rear Admiral John E. Kirkpatrick.

The anchor first found a place downtown, and it was moved in 2006 during the renovations to Campbell Art Park, now home of the Oklahoma Contemporary Arts Center. The monument stands as a vivid reminder of the sacrifices of past generations, the embodiment of John Adams's thought that he must study war so that his sons may study commerce and their children may study art.

STOCK CAR RACES AND PRO GAMES

Where could fans see just about any outdoor sport?

Few folks can remember a time before Taft Stadium, built in 1934 as a WPA project. Seating originally 18,000, the stadium served as the battleground for high school athletics between the highest-ranking schools in the state. Collegiate football came onto the field, too, with Bedlam games between University of Oklahoma (OU) and Oklahoma State University (OSU) held midway between them to save on travel costs during World War II. In 1968, the stadium became professional with Oklahoma City's Continental Football Association team, the Plainsmen, playing there. Things got even bigger in 2015 with the OKC Energy playing their games in the new stadium, which brought attention from national broadcasts.

TAFT STADIUM

WHAT: WPA stadium that has seated many thousands over the years

WHERE: 2501 N May Ave.

COST: Event tickets are usually only a few dollars.

PRO TIP: Check out the satellite view for the monumental "OKC" sign in the stands.

Perhaps the wildest venture at Taft Stadium was the stock car racing of the mid-20th century. A quarter-mile dirt track was installed around the field in 1946. While intended for running, it was perfect for driving cars in frantic, near-continuous turns that made engines rev and spectators howl. For years, Taft was the center of numerous

The 1951 Milk and Ice Fund benefit offered the winner $1,750 for the stock car race as a portion of the proceeds. Thousands more went to charity.

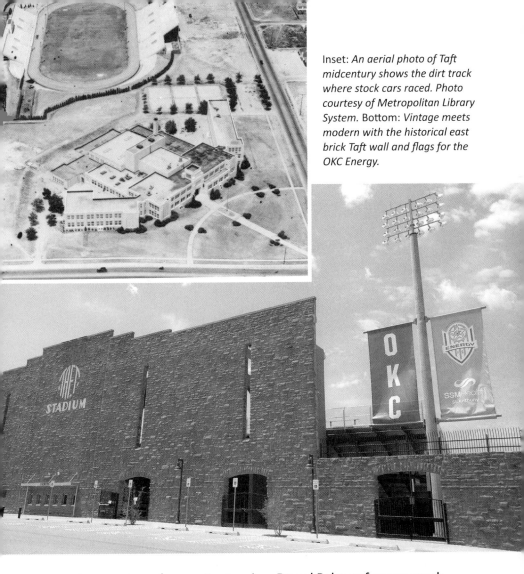

Inset: *An aerial photo of Taft midcentury shows the dirt track where stock cars raced. Photo courtesy of Metropolitan Library System.* Bottom: *Vintage meets modern with the historical east brick Taft wall and flags for the OKC Energy.*

racing events and even stunt racing. Darrel Palmer, former coach and member of the Taft Stadium Board, told *The Oklahoman* about finding eight-millimeter film showing races, with the winner receiving a trophy and a smooch before he went "out the double gate, which is still there, and drove onto May Avenue and took off."

In 2013, Oklahoma City Public Schools announced major renovations that would modernize the stadium. Though the west wall containing graffiti signatures of generations of players who graced the field was lost, contractors were able to save the iconic eastern wall. Just as it has for nearly a century, the red-brick face with the stylized circular "Taft" sign watches over East May today, hinting at generations more of athletes who will test themselves behind it.

THE RISE, FALL, AND RESURRECTION OF AUTOMOBILE ALLEY

Why do they call that stretch of Broadway "Automobile Alley"?

Broadway Avenue is famously wide enough to allow a wagon with a team of horses to turn around without having to back up. Though that was the idea when Oklahoma City began in 1889, it wasn't long after that automobiles took over the roads. Chris Salyer, one of the forces behind today's Automobile Alley, mentioned how every city of consequence had an "automobile alley." This was the district where car dealers of every make lined up to show the latest models in classy, indoor showrooms.

After Pearl Harbor, everything changed. The government put a freeze on consumer car production, and US automakers went from producing 4.7 million automobiles for the public to building tanks, airplanes, and bombs. "That's why you don't see any 1942 Lincolns or 1943 Packards," Salyer explained. Automobile alleys around the country closed up shop, and most were torn down, but Oklahoma City was fortunate to hold onto the poured-concrete buildings with steel supports where cars once waited for new owners.

Salyer remembers a night decades ago, when out with friends downtown, that he stopped and laid in the street at the corner of Main Street and Broadway Avenue. Everyone asked, "What are

Each holiday season, the street glows with Lights on Broadway. Shops do window displays, family-friendly programming lines the sidewalks, and Santa appears inside a giant snow globe for photos.

Bottom: *The Buick Building as it looked in 1912. Photo courtesy of the Metropolitan Library System.* Inset: *Salyer's upstairs car collection, where dealers' vehicles once stood waiting for buyers.*

you doing?" "There's something wrong here," he replied. It should have been one of the busiest intersections in the city, but downtown was dead.

Through the coming years, Salyer and others invested in making downtown come back to life. What had been car dealerships are now restaurants, specialty shops, and loft apartments. Salyer himself lives in one, housing his car collection and using the same car-sized elevators that dealers did, nearly a century ago.

BROADWAY 10 CHOPHOUSE

WHAT: Wood-fired meats and handcrafted cocktails in the historic Buick Building

WHERE: 1101 N Broadway Ave.

COST: Brunch, lunch, and dinner, starting at around $15

PRO TIP: Check out dining on the mezzanine, which was once managers' office space overlooking the showroom floor.

THE MACHINE GUN ON TOP OF BYRON'S

Was there really a gunner's nest set up to guard the liquor warehouse?

Oklahoma ended its 52-year prohibition of hard liquor in 1959, the same year that Byron's Liquor Warehouse opened a few blocks west of the state capitol on 23rd Street. It has long been a staple of the city, as has the legend that there was once a gun tower installed on the roof to defend the store. The supposed reasons *why* there was a tower range from urban riot control to managing busy sales days, so, in 2018, reporter Claire Donnelly of PBS radio station KGOU-FM decided to find out the truth on the local history podcast, *How Curious*.

The story began, as did the store itself, with Byron Gambulos. Born in Dallas to Greek and German immigrants, Gambulos served in the Philippines in World War II before returning to his passion: entrepreneurship. His love of business began early with a hamburger stand at age 10, and, at the end of prohibition, Gambulos was well-prepared to help organize the state's transition to legal liquor by creating store models and showing people how to apply. When one of the stores was forbidden a license due to bootlegging charges, Gambulos took over, and Byron's continues as a family business today.

BYRON'S LIQUOR WAREHOUSE

WHAT: "Oklahoma's #1 destination," per Byron's website

WHERE: 2322 N Broadway Ave.

COST: Drinks range from single-flavor shots for a few dollars to valuable bottles of wine.

PRO TIP: With 30,000 square feet, Byron's is likely to have what you're looking for.

Above these doors, a wooden gunnery tower once stood.

The machine gun came in 1963, when Gambulos refused a cash deal to sell out to a mobster trying to buy up liquor stores. The angry would-be buyer attacked the store with a homemade bomb. Gambulos set up a gunnery tower on the roof and brought his friends in to help keep watch at night. Each brought his own weapons, and Gambulos carried his machine gun from World War II. Their watch one night caught a man preparing a pipe bomb, and they scared him off with warning shots. The bomb left a crater in the street, but the store was safe.

After police caught those responsible for bombing OKC liquor stores, the tower came down in 1965.

How Curious has tackled other Oklahoma City mysteries, such as the disappearing Russian house and why the Lakeview neighborhood doesn't have a view of Lake Hefner.

MILK BOTTLE GROCERY

What's a giant milk bottle doing on top of a building?

US Route 66, the Mother Road, is well known for her wonderfully gimmicky giants. Oklahoma has plenty in its share, from a blue whale in Catoosa to the giant Native American Muffler Man in Calumet, but it doesn't get much better for Oklahoma City residents than the famous Milk Bottle. While advertising alone is often enough of a cause for a roadside attraction, the Milk Bottle came about for an even more practical reason: people had problems finding the place!

Location is everything in business, and establishing a grocery store on one of the prominent intersections in Oklahoma City makes great sense. The problem, however, was that its 350 square feet took up just about every square inch of space on the tiny, triangular block. As bigger buildings went up around it, the grocery had no way of standing out to attract customers. With such limited storefront in three directions, adding a sign tall enough would be problematic; they needed something practically cylindrical. The solution was obvious when it came in 1948: add a huge milk bottle made out of sheet metal atop the building.

Not only did the giant bottle make the store notable, it also served as advertising space. For decades, from 1950 to

---

Before the milk bottle, the building was known as "Triangle Grocery," thanks to its triangular shape at the three-way intersection of Classen Boulevard, Northwest 24th Street, and Military Avenue.

Right: *When the Milk Bottle Building had Townley's stamp. Photo courtesy of John Margolies, Roadside America Archive, Library of Congress.* Inset: *Today, the Milk Bottle Building shows Braum's.*

1980, the stamp of Townley's Dairy. Today it bears the ice-cream-cone logo of the famed Braum's Dairy, one of the largest dairy operations in the world.

The building itself has changed hands several times, serving as everything from a cleaners to a sandwich shop. No matter what's inside, it will always be known as the Milk Bottle Grocery, added to the National Register of Historic Places in 1998 on the bottle's 50th anniversary.

THE BRAUM'S MILK BOTTLE

WHAT: An 11-foot-tall metal milk bottle

WHERE: 2426 N Classen Blvd.

COST: At $4/gallon, that milk bottle would run about $3,450.

PRO TIP: Take a gander south for another Route 66 icon, the Gold Dome Building.

WHERE THE STARS SING

What's the hidden history behind one of OKC's biggest venues?

Nothing showcases the living history of Oklahoma City like the Civic Center. It was born of both wealth and poverty nearly a century ago. In 1927, when Oklahoma City was bursting with cash from oil, voters approved a $4 million bond to buy land west of downtown for a municipal auditorium. Suddenly strapped by the Great Depression, OKC was aided by the federal Public Works Administration, which paid for more than half of the original construction. Together, they created a six-story icon of the arts that blends neoclassical and art deco styles into a place like no other.

The Civic Center has been renovated several times through the years, including major changes to the main theater that brought the Municipal Auditorium into the modern era of the music hall in 1967 and updates with the Metropolitan Area Projects Plan (MAPS) in 1997. Today, the building is packed with spaces, from the

OKC CIVIC CENTER BOX OFFICE

WHAT: The hub for Broadway shows, concerts, and graduations

WHERE: 201 N Walker Ave.

COST: Tickets can range from a few dollars for a matinee play to hundreds as a VIP-Platinum.

PRO TIP: Book a free guided tour for your group to hear 75 years of Civic Center history.

A nine-foot bronze sculpture was installed in 2007 to commemorate of the Oklahoma City Philharmonic's conductors in the visage of Joel Levine, who served for three decades.

Top: *Though much has changed inside, the Civic Center still bears its Depression façade.* Inset: *A bronze conductor gives tribute to those who have led the Oklahoma City Philharmonic.*

2,477-set Thelma Gaylord Performing Arts Theatre, to the 286-seat, classic art deco Freede Little Theatre, to the 90-seat, black-box-style, Cityspace Theatre, not to mention lounges, halls, and suites. In addition to bringing in major national shows, it also serves as the focal point for local opera, ballet, and the Oklahoma City Philharmonic.

The walls of the Civic Center hold a thousand stories, and not just those told onstage through plays, musicals, and ballet. In 1976, young Norman musician Vince Gill got a call for his bluegrass band Mountain Smoke to take over for an opening act that dropped out. He later recalled he thought it must have been for something like a Shriners convention, but when they arrived at the Civic Center, they saw the sign for Kiss as part of its Alive! tour. The rock fans were just as shocked as the bluegrass players, and it nearly sparked a riot before they were taken offstage. The newspaper noted, "Gill on his departure showed the crowd which part of his anatomy the crowd could kiss."

LEAPY THE LEOPARD

What's a city to do with a leopard on the loose?

After moving to Lincoln Park in 1925, the Oklahoma City Zoo rapidly expanded. It was a major WPA project, building an amphitheater still in use today and a bathhouse for swimming; today, the building is home to ZooZeum, packed with zoo history. In 1949, the OKC zoo launched a campaign, "Children's Pennies for a New Elephant," that brought the famed Judy the Elephant to inspire kids for generations. Another campaign in 1953 was launched after OKC-native Gayla Peevey released "I Want a Hippopotamus for Christmas." Everybody in OKC agreed and sent in dimes, funding Matilda the hippo to join the zoo.

In 1950, Oklahoma City gained national attention upon the arrival of two Indian leopards. The male, Luther, earned the nickname "Leapy" when he made a miraculous 22-foot vertical jump out of the big cat pit and escaped the zoo. For the next three days, Leapy was loose, and the city

OKLAHOMA CITY ZOO

WHAT: More than 1,900 animals on 120 acres, including great apes, elephants, and Oklahoma critters

WHERE: 2101 NE 50th St.

COST: $12 for adults, $9 for children and seniors

PRO TIP: Group rates are available, making it a great outing for a birthday or class party!

History almost replayed itself in 1953 when another leopard slipped out of her cage, but staff brought her down before she made it off zoo property.

Top: *A 1945 postcard shows leopard pride at the zoo.* Inset: *Another relic of the Oklahoma City Zoo was the ship-themed Monkey Island. Photos courtesy of the Metropolitan Library System*

went nuts. Hundreds of volunteers turned out to comb the city, block by block. The National Guard and Marines arrived alongside dozens of big-cat hunters and their dogs. *Life Magazine* estimated some 3,000 people joined the hunt.

Finally, Leapy was found napping just a few yards from the zoo gate. He had circled back, eaten drugged horsemeat left out as bait, and fallen into a stupor. Despite wild tales of attempted attacks all over the city, Leapy had likely been hiding and unable to eat; when he got to the horsemeat, he ate too much of the tranquilizers and later passed away in his sleep. The city was brokenhearted at the sad fate of the leopard that had caused so much excitement, and he received more than 1,200 letters from his fans. He was stuffed and mounted, returning to the zoo statuesque to again bring his audiences to marvel at the wonders of nature.

SIT-INS AGAINST SEGREGATION

Who started the sit-in at Katz Drug Store?

In 1958, Clara Shepard Luper took the group of students she was mentoring in the National Association for the Advancement of Colored People (NAACP) Youth Council on a trip to the East Coast. When they returned, Luper's eight-year-old daughter suggested that they go get a Coke on a hot August day, just as they had when they were back east. Luper had contacted Katz Drug Store many times, but in Oklahoma City, it continued to be a whites-only soda parlor. With the Youth Council's consensus, she coordinated the sit-in to desegregate the city.

Luper was no stranger to doing what it took to find justice. After receiving her bachelor's degree from Langston University, she was one of a group that applied to the then-segregated University of Oklahoma (OU) to challenge unfair race laws. The group won its case, and Luper was the first African American admitted to the graduate History program at OU. She graduated with her master's in 1951 and taught history in John Marshall and Classen high schools.

KAISER'S GRATEFUL BEAN CAFÉ

WHAT: A classic ice cream parlor, complete with marble counter

WHERE: 1039 N Walker Ave.

COST: Coffees under $2, sundaes and floats for $5, and burgers for $12

PRO TIP: Check out tons of ice cream flavors, and take a one-pound carton of homemade ice cream to go!

The Oklahoma City sit-in was one of several precursors to the famed Greensboro, North Carolina, sit-in that sparked nationwide sit-ins in 1960 to promote desegregation.

Top: *Kaiser's in Oklahoma City opened just three years after the Katz chain started in Kansas.* Inset: *The historical counter at Kaiser's shows the stature soda parlors carry.*

Luper and the kids walked to Katz Drug Store downtown and ordered Cokes. They were refused service, but they remained on the stools in a quiet demand for fair service. Oklahoma City police watched over the scene, which remained nonviolent despite jeering threats from some offended whites. Finally, they were served, and Luper would go on to lead the desegregation of restaurants, hotels, and theaters throughout the city.

The Katz Drug Store where it all went down was demolished in the Pei Plan restructuring of downtown, but on the 60th anniversary of the sit-in, another Oklahoma City icon stepped up to help commemorate the memory. Kaiser's Grateful Bean Café continues the ice cream parlor tradition in the same place where Swiss immigrant Tony Kaiser set up his shop in 1917. In 2018, a crowd reenacted the march by going from Frontline Church to Kaiser's, where they were all welcomed and served, showing the best of history and progress together.

SHOWING YOUR STUFF

Who's the greatest Oklahoma athlete of all time?

Mickey Mantle grew up in Commerce, Oklahoma, and Jim Thorpe was raised near Prague, but Oklahoma City's own is Johnny Bench, born in 1947. Bench headed out of town to join the Cincinnati Reds for 17 years, collecting an enormous swath of awards: two World Series rings, four pennants, six division titles, MVP in 1970 and 1972, and MVP of the 1976 World Series with an incredible .533 batting average. He's often called the greatest one-handed catcher of all time (he kept the other hand behind his back to protect it for throwing), and, in 1989, the very first year that he was eligible for the Baseball Hall of Fame, he was voted in with the third-highest total of votes in history.

Today, Bench is immortalized with his own statue and plaza right in the heart of Bricktown, on the southwest end of the ballpark. His is one of many bronze memorials along the trail on Mickey Mantle Drive, including famed two-way player Wilbert "Bullet Joe" Rogan and Allie Reynolds of the Creek Nation, graduate of Capitol Hill High School.

For more flavor of Oklahoma's finesse in fitness, head upstairs to the Oklahoma Sports Hall of Fame. Much of the museum is dedicated to Jim Thorpe, who was pronounced the greatest athlete in the world by Sweden's King Gustav V after Thorpe's sweep of gold medals in the 1912 Olympics. Cases of memorabilia

The Sports Hall of Fame also offers a series of community advocacy programs under the organization "Bright Path," which is the English translation of Jim Thorpe's Sauk name, Wa-tho-huk.

Top: *The statue of Johnny Bench stands over his namesake plaza.* Bottom: *Inside the museum, learn the history of the world's greatest athlete, Jim Thorpe.*

detail Thorpe's life, successes, and struggles overcoming racism, such as his medals being stripped away before ultimately they were restored in 1982.

The hall of fame is a trove of treasures from every angle of Oklahoma athletics. Guests can view gymnast Shannon Miller's wrist guards, Jim Shoulders's rodeo spurs, and Sean O'Grady's gloves, which he wore as the World Boxing Association lightweight champion of 1981.

OKLAHOMA SPORTS HALL OF FAME & JIM THORPE MUSEUM

WHAT: A showcase of Oklahoma's greatest athletes

WHERE: 20 S Mickey Mantle Dr.

COST: Free

PRO TIP: Keep an eye out for relics from Oklahoma sports heroes in wrestling, boxing, and tennis.

131

TASTES OF BRAZIL

Have you tried *virado* (pork chop, sausage, eggs, kale, pork rind, rice, and beans) in an old funeral parlor?

In 2005, Ana Davis opened a restaurant to fulfill her dream of a place that tasted and felt like Brazil—"colorful, happy, and loud in many ways." She and her brother had been operating More than Muffins on Classen Boulevard for 10 years previously. The opportunity to expand was an exciting one, especially in such a beautiful Spanish Revival building in the heart of Midtown, across from the Plaza Court. Davis said that she fell in love with the high-ceilinged chapel. It reminded her of a restaurant she had visited in Spain inside a converted chapel, and she wanted to share that feeling with her customers.

Renovations over the course of a year turned the chapel into a vibrant dining room. The walls are painted blue and yellow, the colors of the Brazilian flag, and folk art and live plants serve as decorations. The food served up is authentically Brazilian from the *feijoada brasileira* (Brazilian black bean stew) to the *xin-xin* (chicken and shrimp with palm oil, coconut milk, cashews,

CAFÉ DO BRAZIL

WHAT: Brazilian cuisine in a remodeled funeral parlor

WHERE: 440 NW 11th St.

COST: Lunches for $10 and up, dinner for $20 and up

PRO TIP: Try the Dinner For Two with a wide variety of meats and vegetables, along with dessert.

In addition to the dining rooms on the main floor, the café offers patio seating and the Bossa Nova Bar upstairs, with views of the Oklahoma City skyline.

132

Café do Brazil's classy Spanish Revival exterior was established by the Garrisons years before.

peanut paste, and fresh herbs). Chef Ana herself was born in Belo Horizonte and returns to Brazil annually to cook alongside chefs, to keep her skills sharp.

The story of Café do Brazil is fascinating enough, yet there is more to the building's tale. This was the old Garrison Funeral Home. Maurice and Elizabeth Garrison operated the funeral home until their retirement in 1978, and continued to live in the apartment above until Mrs. Garrison's passing. They were both active in numerous Oklahoma City community organizations, and Mrs. Garrison is said to be the first woman to be granted a funeral director's license in Oklahoma. The legend is that Mrs. Garrison's spirit checks in on the place and has been very pleased with how Ana Davis has given the building new life.

PEI'S PLAN

Did they really demolish half of downtown?

The 1950s were a tough time for downtown Oklahoma City. Low oil prices meant there wasn't as much money around, and there were more cars than ever to give the option of moving out to cheaper areas on the outskirts of town. Many of the buildings sat empty, attracting vagrants. Then, city leaders had a plan, or, actually, they approved a plan, by famed architect I. M. Pei.

Pei had just finished an urban redesign in Cleveland, and OKC thought it was about time to do the same. The first part of the Pei Plan was to tear down all the dilapidated buildings, as well as any that got in the way of finally straightening those crooked streets from 1889. This cleared out 40 percent of downtown, with block after block of demolition. Some buildings weren't missed, but others like the palatial Baum building and the towering Biltmore Hotel left gaps in the Oklahoma City skyline to this day.

The second step of the plan was to throw open the doors to developers to put in shopping and apartments around a central park. Once people came, streets would convert to pedestrian malls, and . . . it never happened. Instead, downtown was seen as eerily empty, and developers and citizens alike continued to move away to fresher parts of the city. It wouldn't be until the Metropolitan Area Projects Plan (MAPS) projects of the 1990s that downtown would really start to turn around.

MYRIAD BOTANICAL GARDENS

WHAT: 17 acres of parkland in the heart of the city

WHERE: 301 W Reno Ave.

COST: Admission to the Crystal Bridge Tropical Conservatory is $8 and under.

PRO TIP: Park for free on the south end and walk a couple of blocks to avoid McGee's legacy, the parking meter.

134

Left: *Midway through urban renewal, gaps were already appearing downtown. Photo courtesy of the Metropolitan Library System.* Inset: *Even in winter, the Myriad Gardens sparkle with the tropics inside. Photo courtesy of Dennis Spielman*

Though the Pei Plan didn't come to fruition as hoped, it did give Oklahoma City its first convention center and the Myriad Gardens. Opened in 1988, the Myriad Botanical Gardens welcomes more than two million visitors a year to ride the carousel, ice-skate in the winter, and enjoy a rainforest experience inside the Crystal Bridge.

After the Pei Plan opened park space, the ultramodernist Mummers Theater, also known as Stage Center, blossomed downtown for a few years before being torn down in 2013.

THE TUNNELS

Were there really hundreds of people living beneath downtown?

The story goes that there were once tunnels running under Oklahoma City, stretching for blocks, and that story is absolutely true!

Though legendary today, the Chinese Tunnels were commonly known a century ago. Oklahoma City had its own Chinatown, with immigrant workers who built up a neighborhood at what is now the Myriad Botanical Gardens. Hemmed in by minority laws, the Chinese citizens expanded their living space by digging basements, sub-basements, and sub-sub-basements that were linked by hallways and tunnels under the street. Newspapers reported some 200 people living below ground at its peak. When downtown declined in the 1940s, people moved out.

The tunnels were rediscovered in 1969 with the demolitions of the Pei Plan. Bulldozers turned up one concrete room after the other. "Mr. Oklahoma History" and former mayor, George Shirk, led an urban exploration party into the tunnels, taking photographs of kitchens, bedrooms, and laundries. Then, those rooms were demolished, too.

There are some tall tales about the Chinese Tunnels running all the way up to the Gold Dome on Northwest 23rd Street and south past the river. No one is quite sure how far they did run, but during construction of the new convention center parking garage in 2019,

OKC UNDERGROUND

WHAT: Over a mile of twisting tunnels

WHERE: Stretching from the Dowell Center on NW 4th St. and Harvey Ave. to the Prairie Surf Studios parking at Sheridan Ave. and Broadway Ave., with entrances all in between

COST: Free

NOTABLE: Tunnels are open Monday through Friday, 6 a.m. to 8 p.m., making it a great way to get around without getting into the weather.

Top: *George Shirk leads an expedition into the uncovered dwelling spaces in 1969. Photo courtesy of* The Oklahoman. Inset: *The OKC Underground today. Courtesy of Dennis Spielman*

workers were baffled when they dug up rotten support beams far deeper than anything should have been.

Though the Chinese Tunnels are gone, there is a new system of tunnels that runs beneath downtown. Built in 1974 and originally named the "Conncourse" for OKC businessman Jack Conn, the tunnels link up numerous hotels, parking lots, and towers downtown for easy pedestrian traffic. Each section of the tunnels is lit in a thematic color and offers art galleries showing local history and works by invited artists.

For a different view of town, check out the skywalks off the Oklahoma Tower at Park and Harvey avenues and the Renaissance Hotel at Sheridan and Broadway avenues.

THE GREAT ANNEXATION

Why Is Oklahoma City so BIG?

Oklahoma City is huge, bigger even than Houston and Los Angeles! With minimal traffic on the highways, it can take upwards of an hour to drive from end to end, whether from McLoud in the east to Yukon in the west or Norman in the south to Edmond in the north. Folks like to say that it's the open spaces of the rolling prairie that makes Oklahoma Citians like to spread out, but our wide city limits actually tie into eager politics and wishful thinking.

Stanley Draper was known as "Mr. Chamber of Commerce" in Oklahoma City. Born the same year as the Land Run, Draper came to Oklahoma City in 1919 as a veteran of World War I and found work as the membership secretary for the chamber of commerce. This began his 49-year career as a professional booster for the city, with 38 years as managing director for the chamber. He worked to move railroad tracks, bring in the Federal Aviation Administration (FAA) training center and OU Health

LAKE STANLEY DRAPER

WHAT: OKC's third reservoir, named for city booster Stanley Draper

WHERE: 8301 SE 104th St.

COST: Rent your own piece of OKC land for camping for $8/night

PRO TIP: This is OKC's only lake that allows waterskiing, so ski it up!

As of the 2010 census, Oklahoma City is the eighth-largest US city in area. Most "larger" cities in Alaska and Montana have much smaller populations, although #5 Jacksonville has 240,000 more people in 141 more square miles.

Left: *Stanley Draper's statue stands outside city hall in commemoration of all his efforts as a booster for OKC.* Right: *Portrait of Stanley Draper. Photo courtesy of the Oklahoma Hall of Fame*

Sciences Center, and set up a reservoir with a pipeline to Lake Atoka for plenty of water.

Draper was also one of the forces behind the Great Annexation of 1959. After years of work to establish Tinker Air Force Base only to see the surrounding area incorporate separately as Midwest City, OKC leaders decided to bring in every square mile of land they could, despite smaller communities balking. In 1959, the city was 68 square miles. Within 24 months, the city had expanded to 475. Four more years brought another 174 square miles to Oklahoma City, now half the size of Rhode Island.

There were some obvious growing pains. Just a few months in, the new city map was too tall to fit the ceilings at city hall. Oklahoma City became responsible for more than 1,000 old wooden bridges and dirt roads, while its police were stretched thin covering the area. It later trimmed down to today's svelte 606 square miles.

SKELETONS!

Who would've thought "bonehead" is such a great compliment?

It all started when seven-year-old Jay Villemarette discovered a dog skull in the woods and developed a lifelong passion for bones. After earning awards at science fairs in school, he turned cleaning and selling skulls into a hobby. The hobby grew into a part-time job, and the part-time job grew into Skulls Unlimited, a company known the world over for its quality skulls and skeletons. In 2000, Villemarette went even further, to share a collection of more than 300 skeletons of all kinds in a place unlike any other, a Museum of Osteology.

The museum is more than just storage space, although even that would be impressive. Each skeleton is arranged in lifelike poses, showing how the bone structures of the body work. Skeletons in the museum range from tiny mice and birds all the way up to the big guys, such as giraffes, a rhinoceros, and several full whales hanging overhead. Comparative exhibits

SKELETONS: MUSEUM OF OSTEOLOGY

WHAT: A two-level museum showcasing more than 300 skeletons

WHERE: 10301 S Sunnylane Rd.

COST: $11 for adults, $9 for kids, and free for 3 and under

PRO TIP: Check out special events, such as forensics classes showing how bone science solves mysteries.

Virtually every skeleton in the museum is the real thing. The handful of replicas are marked with red dots to ensure the bones stand out as impressively as they are in real life.

Top: *Articulated skeletons of all kinds are posed as if in motion at the Museum of Osteology.* Inset: *Measure yourself up against the giant skull of a whale.*

explain invertebrates and vertebrates, how the shell of a turtle works, and why some birds fly and some don't, all with real skeletal examples plain to see. Before visiting, people might not be able to describe how bones figure into locomotion, with longer ones used for hopping and shorter ones for waddling, but they certainly will understand after seeing the skeletons frozen in action!

In addition to seeing skeletons, guests have an opportunity at the Explorer's Corner for hands-on experience with different kinds of bones, as well as quizzes to test what they've learned. Other exhibits show the fascinating methods of skeleton-cleaning, using dermestid beetles and chemical baths. Then, in the gift shop, pick up a skull of your own to take home!

EXOTIC ANIMAL RACING

Ever seen a camel race?

Remington Park has been racing quarter horses and thoroughbreds before excited Oklahoma City crowds since 1988. Owned by the Chickasaw Nation, it serves as the premier site for horseracing in the state with two graded events, the Oklahoma Derby and the Remington Park Oaks. Racers come from all over the world to participate, dreaming of six-figure purses.

The facility was rated as the third-best racetrack in the world by the Horseplayers Association in 2009. It was actually a novel experiment when it began, with its track being laid using a waterproof, wax-polymer coating on sand grains to attempt to create an all-weather surface. Although the brutal Oklahoma summer did not suit the wax, it put Oklahoma City on the world racing map. Most people who attend look forward to horse races, mud runs along a three-mile obstacle course, and even motorcycle events, but Remington offers something a little more extreme each April.

Extreme Racing Day brings out the unexpected animals for fun competitions that gather crowds upwards of 25,000 people. The most famous four-legged participants are camels and zebras, which are brought in from worldwide racing institutions. There are also racing ostriches, specially trained to carry a rider upwards of 25 miles per hour. In addition,

Each winning animal is partnered with a charity, ranging from literacy to special needs to foster care, which receives a $1,000 donation from Remington Park.

Left: *Ostriches, camels, and more race at Remington Park.* Right: *A zebra crosses the finish line on Extreme Racing Day. Photos by Dustin Orona Photography, courtesy of Remington Park*

Remington offers miniature donkey races to show the smallest of the small, and features the biggest of the big with Clydesdales, the enormous workhorses that can stand more than six feet tall. Each Extreme Racing day is a little different, depending on what animals are available for racing, but spectators can be sure to raise their eyebrows at the unfamiliar creatures showing their physical prowess as they tear around the track.

REMINGTON PARK EXTREME RACE DAY FOR CHARITY

WHAT: Enjoy races with exotic animals such as camels, zebras, and ostriches.

WHERE: 1 Remington Pl.

COST: Free

PRO TIP: The event usually takes place on a Sunday in April, so mark your calendars!

WRONG TO CALL IT A "PET CEMETERY"

What museum offers final resting grounds for famous animals?

The National Cowboy & Western Heritage Museum is no secret. Its halls are packed with artifacts and paintings from the American West, both long ago and today. It has brought millions to Oklahoma City since opening in 1955. What folks might not know about it is that the grounds are the final resting place for a host of Western animals.

"It would be wrong to call it a 'pet cemetery,'" according to McCasland Chair of Cowboy Culture and Curator, Michael R. Grauer. The animals here were not pets at all, but part of the menagerie that has impressed spectators for decades. It began with Abilene, the longhorn "mascot" of the museum in its early days. When he passed, staff decided to bury him on-site among the many memorials in the gardens and sculptures on museum

The story of the West had a lot more players than the stereotypes shown in old Westerns. Check out inspiring stories of women, minorities, and native peoples among the museum's exhibits.

Top: *The marker for Abilene, the cowboy museum's longtime mascot.*
Inset: *The marker for the nearly unrideable Tornado.*

property. He had a simple wooden sign, fitting for a humble yet impressive bull that had dropped so many jaws over the years. Soon, others came to join him, including the broncs Midnight and Five Minutes Til Midnight, who were disinterred to be laid to rest at the museum.

Most famous of all is Tornado. Henryetta rancher Jim Shoulders raised up the bucking bull, who seemed to be completely unrideable. Though Shoulders's daughters could feed Tornado cookies by hand, no one could hold on when he bucked. For seven years, rider after rider tried and failed to stay on top. It wasn't until 1967 at the National Finals Rodeo that 46-year-old Freckles Brown, who faced competitors half his age, managed to wear Tornado out in what he called the greatest moment of his life.

When Tornado died five years later, he was granted a funeral worthy of royalty and laid to rest before a crowd of men in black, holding their cowboy hats to their chests in respect.

LITTLE SAIGON

Have you heard the story of Oklahoma City's Vietnamese population?

Oklahoma City's original Chinatown on the southern end of downtown vanished with the decline of the center of the city in the mid-1900s, but only a few decades later, a new Asian population arrived to revitalize the area around the old railway line up Classen Boulevard. San Nguyen was a part-time translator at the US Embassy in Saigon during the Vietnam War. After the fall of South Vietnam, he was one of those evacuated by helicopter from the embassy roof. He arrived in America with thousands of other refugees outside of Fort Smith. Through his work and of others in the nonprofit group Catholic Charities, he found sponsors in Oklahoma City that would bring more than 7,000 families to town.

Hardworking entrepreneurs soon turned the struggling area around. A low cost of living and opportunities for employment brought people to live in houses that had long sat empty. Storefronts reopened with bakeries and restaurants, many offering secret menus with traditional Vietnamese cuisine in addition to their posted food items that were largely recognizable Chinese-American dishes. Parents worked multiple shifts to encourage children in their education, which has produced a wealth of dentists, physicians, accountants, and lawyers throughout the neighborhood.

Many of the older refugees will tell their stories, such as Loc Le, who lost his entire business in the war. He spent his remaining money to buy a small boat and escaped to sea with as many people as it

---

Military Park was originally named after the Oklahoma State Military Institute by developer I. M. Putnam. Today it is fittingly tied to the heroes of the Vietnam War.

Top: *The stylized southern entrance to the Asian District.* Inset: *A memorial to American and South Vietnamese soldiers of the Vietnam War.*

could carry. The crew of a freighter offered them water, but Le refused to be left behind, clinging to the freighter's anchor line and telling them, "Take us aboard or we'll die." Le arrived in the United States in 1975 and, after years of work, bought a café known as Jimmy's Egg that has since grown to more than 60 locations.

Today, the Asian District is known as a foodie hotspot, offering dozens of pho restaurants and specialty eateries. The Super Cao Nguyen supermarket opened in 1979, and continues to be a source for international groceries not often seen on typical grocery store chain shelves.

PHO CA DAO

WHAT: One of the first Vietnamese restaurants in Oklahoma City

WHERE: 2431 N Classen Blvd.

COST: Very affordable, with pho bowls running under $10

PRO TIP: The website OK Gourmet recommends the Chicken Bún as a must-try item.

SONIC BOOMS AND SONIC CUPS

Have you heard the "sonic" in Sonic came from sonic booms?

In 1964, Oklahoma City was picked as the testing ground for supersonic transportation (SST) flights. Engineers had overcome the structural issues of breaking the sound barrier with craft that could withstand the intense compression. A new problem had come up: the enormous bang as the pressure waves broke free from the craft when it passed the sound barrier was worse than thunder. Would people stand for noise loud enough to shake the walls to realize dreams of supersonic air travel? Oklahoma Citians experienced it and voted "no."

At first, Oklahoma City was excited to be the center of prestige for such a test, and the fact was touted by city boosters such as Stanley Draper. Then, every day for months at scheduled times, sonic booms would rain down over the city. A 300-page report from the National Opinion Research Center noted 94 percent of people reporting "rattles and

---

SONIC DRIVE-IN AND GIANT CUP

WHAT: One of Sonic's 3,500 locations

WHERE: 7500 S Choctaw Rd.

COST: If filled with iced tea, that cup would cost about $1,400.

PRO TIP: Hit up happy hour from 2–4 p.m. for half-price drinks and snacks.

The giant Sonic cup off Choctaw Road is actually a cleverly disguised water storage tank, making it perfect for a picture while stretching your legs on a road trip!

Left: *Sonic headquarters overlooking the Bricktown Canal.* Inset: *The enormous Sonic cup overlooking Choctaw Road.*

vibrations." Over the course of three months, annoyance grew from 37 percent to 54 percent, and one-fifth of people claimed damages. The dreams of leaping across continents in mere hours were shattered like a glass frame falling off the wall.

Supersonic travel may have gone out of style, but that didn't stop Troy Smith from success with his fast-food restaurant. In 1954, he had adapted his Top Hat Drive-In in Shawnee to use intercom speakers for service. As the restaurant chain expanded, the name was problematic because it was being copyrighted elsewhere. So, in 1959, it picked a new name and slogan: Sonic, to give "Service with the Speed of Sound." That is fast enough, since no one wants their car rocked by a sonic boom while they get their cherry limeade.

COUNTRY, ROCK, AND METAL

What venue has seen music evolve for six decades?

Few venues in the world can attest to such a variety as the Diamond Ballroom, where Interstate 240 and Interstate 35 meet. Opened in 1964, it has featured everyone from country legend Bob Willis to rocker Peter Frampton, heavy metal band Megadeth, and hip hop group Insane Clown Posse.

In *Diamond Ballroom: From Country Swing to Heavy Metal*, Vernon L. Gowdy III details how the ballroom came to be, from fellas in Oklahoma City pooling their resources to create an institution with Perry Jones and the Diamondaires as the house band. Oklahoma City was largely a dance venue for country music, bringing to the stage stars such as Conway Twitty. But the ballroom has always been innovative, changing with the times as did routine performer Willie Nelson, who played twice in 1968 as a straitlaced member of the Record Men, and Wanda Jackson, who sang at the Diamond long before becoming the Queen of Rockabilly. The ballroom ran a TV show on Saturday nights in the 1960s and often brought in early rock and roll performers such as Fats Domino and Jerry Lee Lewis.

Things took a sudden turn in 1986, when Powerlord played the Diamond Ballroom as its first heavy metal act. It was a bold experiment, turning a Friday night over to a new genre, and crowds were so excited that they brought Powerlord back for a Halloween performance. Soon, more heavy metal and rock by

Through the years, the Diamond has hosted more than just music, including the World Wide Church, funeral services, and union meetings.

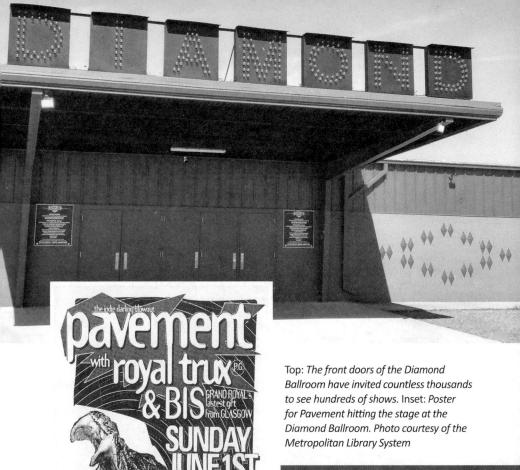

Top: *The front doors of the Diamond Ballroom have invited countless thousands to see hundreds of shows.* Inset: *Poster for Pavement hitting the stage at the Diamond Ballroom. Photo courtesy of the Metropolitan Library System*

DIAMOND BALLROOM

WHAT: Shows across the musical genres for generations

WHERE: 8001 S Eastern Ave.

COST: Tickets are generally $10 and up, with bundles available for table seating

PRO TIP: There are no age restrictions, so some shows might be great for young music lovers but others not so much.

the Furies had the stage on Friday nights, while country swing dominated Saturdays. Such a radical shift might have torn apart other venues, but the Diamond kept it all in step, with pierced, torn T-shirt rockers and boots-and-hat cowboys treating each other like family.

MANY MISS AMERICAS

How many winners have come out of Oklahoma City University?

Oklahoma has been at the forefront of Miss America winners since the beginning. Norma Smallwood from Bristow brought home the sixth-ever title in 1926 as the first person of native heritage to win. Many more Oklahoma ladies, blending elegance and talent, would follow with wins of their own. As of 2020, Oklahoma is tied with California and Ohio for second place with six Miss Americas (New York holds first place). That's impressive enough, but even more so is that three of the ladies came out of a single school: Oklahoma City University (OCU).

Listed as one of the best performing arts schools in the nation, OCU has generated so many pageant winners that the school has assembled a "Hall of Queens" in the Kirkpatrick Fine Arts Center. Portraits of more than 60 of those with highest honors are massed together with titles at state and, of course, national levels. For the Miss America pageant, Jane Anne Jayroe won in 1967, Susan Powell in 1981, and Shawntel Smith in 1995, all with vocal talents refined at OCU.

Hardly one to rest on its laurels, OCU has strived to continue supporting winners with coursework and the Miss OCU Competition. Founded in 1981, the program is designed to help students earn scholarships and education opportunities through winning pageants. Tony- and Emmy-winner Kristin Chenoweth won Miss OCU in 1991.

OKLAHOMA CITY UNIVERSITY PERFORMING ARTS ACADEMY

WHAT: Summer music programs and private instruction

WHERE: 2501 N Blackwelder Ave.

COST: Varies by activity

PRO TIP: Reach out for information on financial aid and scholarships.

Top: *The Hall of Queens shows winners from dozens of high-level pageants.* Inset: *Three Miss Americas smile on the OCU campus.*

It's not just the contestants who are affiliated with the college. Alumnus Chris Harrison came to OCU on a soccer scholarship. His athletics evolved into sportscasting on Oklahoma City TV, which then turned to acting and hosting reality television in Los Angeles, California. In addition to work as the longtime host of *The Bachelor* shows, he has led the entertainment at the Miss America Pageant 17 times.

OCU has had a varied past, including at one point being in Guthrie at the former state capital. Its former names have included Oklahoma Methodist University, Oklahoma City College, and Epworth University.

THE LEGEND OF LITTLE CAREY

Have you heard the spooky story of the Oklahoma City Hatchet House?

There's a small neighborhood in Oklahoma City that resembles something out of a Stephen King novel. The houses are big and glamorous, yet they are all placed together on a narrow strip of road set at an odd angle, almost as if they're from another world. It's called "Carey Place," supposedly named for the girl brutally murdered there.

The story goes that little Carey was up at Gatewood Elementary playing on the swings one cloudy day, when a man with a crazed look in his eye began walking toward her. "Run," he said, taking a hatchet from his overcoat pocket. "I'm gunna kill ya."

Carey ran down the street, turning to pound on her neighbors' doors, one after the other. No one was home, either at work or at school. Finally, the crazed man caught her with his hatchet at one of the driveways and then dragged her to the porch of the Hatchet House to finish her off. To this day, that driveway and

Carey Place has another legend, too, about a window that was shot during a drive-by gangster assassination: whenever the pane is replaced, the bullet hole reappears.

154

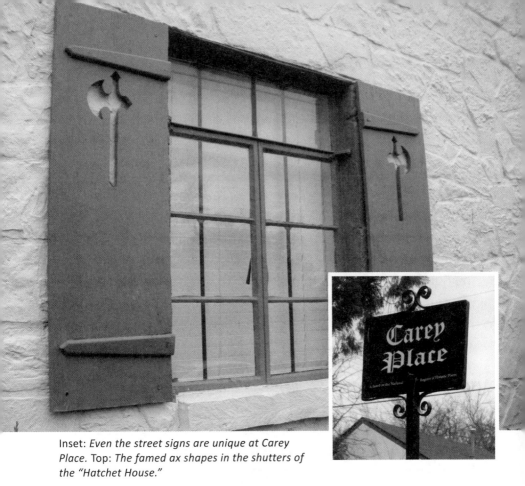

Inset: *Even the street signs are unique at Carey Place.* Top: *The famed ax shapes in the shutters of the "Hatchet House."*

porch are painted red; bloodstains would seep through any other color they tried.

The true story of the name Carey is much more mundane: William P. Carey started his lumber company in 1881 and made good money supplying the wood needed to build Oklahoma City after the Land Run. The neighborhood's land had been intended as a spur of the Oklahoma Railway Company up to Oklahoma City University, but it was never built. Instead, in the 1930s, it became a neighborhood of custom-built homes, including Carey's own house, the one with the turret at the top of the block.

Instead of trying to fight the urban legend, the folks on Carey Place have embraced it as a fun (if gruesome) hook for Halloween. The whole neighborhood dresses up, with even the signposts being redubbed "Scarey Place." Crowds of thousands come out to trick-or-treat.

OSLER BUILDING

What building in Oklahoma City is named after a Canadian doctor?

One of the most iconic representations of Spanish Colonial Revival architectural style rests at the top of Midtown, right here in Oklahoma City. Its blond tapestry brick, U-shaped design of a withdrawn entry inside a court highlighted with decorative concrete recesses is reminiscent of missions across the Southwest and palatial homes in Spain. The best part . . . you can stay there!

The famed six-and-some-floors building began in 1928 as an office building for the Physicians Holding Company, as Midtown grew into the first major medical center for the city. The physicians named it the Osler Building after Sir William Osler, the man who invented residency programs and one of the founders of Johns Hopkins Hospital. It was valuable office space, especially as it had ample parking in a town that only a few years before had been designed for horses. By 1929, with three more floors added on top, the Osler Building housed the Balyeat Allergy Clinic, three dentists, and 35 medical specialists, quite a feat when only 20 percent of doctors nationwide were specialists.

As Oklahoma City hit its downswing in the midcentury and medical research moved eastward to the Health Sciences Center, the Osler Building was vacated in 1965. It sat empty

Osler scandalously called pneumonia "friend of the aged" because it was a relatively quick end compared to enfeebled lingering. Fittingly, Osler died of pneumonia at the age of 70.

Top: *Today, the Ambassador Hotel sits right on the streetcar line.* Inset: *The intricate details of the entry still show on the old Osler Building.*

AMBASSADOR HOTEL

WHAT: Boutique luxury hotel in Midtown

WHERE: 1200 N Walker Ave.

COST: Comfortable rooms around $200/night

PRO TIP: Being right on the streetcar line gives you access all over downtown OKC.

for decades until being reborn as the Ambassador Hotel. The building was renovated into 54 modern guestrooms, placed on the National Register of Historic Places, and opened in 2014 under the guidance of Tulsa developer Paul Coury. Its rooftop bar and balcony offer one of the best views of the rolling Oklahoma City skyline anywhere in town.

THE CURIOUS CASE OF REVEREND DOLAN

Will we ever know what happened to the Bingo King?

Built by the Brothers of Mercy in 1945 and later expanded, the building served as a long-term care facility for the aged and mentally ill. Like other asylums named after St. Vincent, patron saint of charity, the home housed only men, said to range in age from seven to 90. Legends grew up around the facility about a nurse who suffocated two patients and pushed another down the stairs. The nurse turned himself over to police in 1962 and proved to have his own mental illness.

The biggest mystery about St. Vincent's centers around one of its operators, the Rev. Richard Frank Dolan. He had come to Oklahoma City in 1967, assigned by the Roman Catholic Church to establish The Main Artery, an alcohol recovery program. Dolan later earned the nickname "Bingo King" as he organized numerous bingo halls around town,

Though it's easy to focus on scary tales, much good was done taking care of folks who needed care through the years at St. Vincent's.

Top: *The long brick dormitory of St. Vincent's still stands.* Bottom: *Today, graffiti marks one of the entrances to St. Vincent's. Photos courtesy of Abandoned Oklahoma*

as well as some notoriety after he was arrested for soliciting an undercover vice police officer. In 1988, Dolan was discovered dead in his apartment near St. Vincent's, which had been ransacked. As police investigated, it was revealed that Dolan had been attacked several times before, usually in robbery attempts of bingo money, but he had never turned in the attackers because he had said he knew them. The mystery of who killed Dolan remains unsolved.

Today, the building is notorious for legend-trippers hoping they'll see a ghost inside. It remains under police surveillance to deter trespassing. Fortunately, Oklahoma City has plenty of other places to see a ghost.

GHOST CAUGHT ON TAPE!

Was there really a specter in south Oklahoma City?

Late at night on July 18, 2002, Kathy Henley was watching the security surveillance cameras at Puckett's Towing on Southwest 29th Street, when she saw someone on her screens. She radioed her coworker, saying, "Colonel, look, it looks like somebody running across the lot." Then, she corrected herself, "Look, it's floating."

Staff did a thorough search of the lot and came up baffled. The alarms on the fence were all on, and other cameras showed no one entering or exiting. No one was there, and yet someone had been clearly caught on tape. From the spooky nature of the video and the fact that at least three vehicles on the lot that night had been involved in lethal accidents, folks soon began coming to the conclusion that it was a ghost.

Word got around to news stations, and soon Oklahoma City was making international headlines. Copies of the video were played throughout the world, clearly showing a figure walking among wrecked vehicles. Paranormal investigators concluded that it was likely a woman who died nearly three weeks earlier, checking

OKLAHOMA CITY GHOST TOUR

WHAT: A walk around Bricktown and downtown OKC, featuring spooky historical stories

WHERE: 101 E Sheridan Ave.

COST: $12

PRO TIP: Check out facebook.com/AuthorJeffProvine for event dates.

Numerous paranormal shows have tackled the Puckett's ghost video, including *My Ghost Story*, National Geographic's *Is It Real?*, and *Caught on Camera*.

Top: *Puckett's Towing on Southwest 29th Street with its classy, midcentury sign.*
Bottom: *A still of the ghost caught on tape. Photo courtesy of Chris Puckett*

back on the spot where her car had been until that afternoon, when it was taken away for processing by the insurance company. Many cried, "Hoax!", and a special effects team in Los Angeles, California managed to re-create the video using their years of experience and thousands of dollars of equipment.

The original tape has been erased, after Puckett's was so inundated with requests from people wanting to see it that it interfered with business. That isn't to say the video is gone forever: it lives on in numerous copies and online streaming videos, and a GIF of the image is available on the Puckett's Inc. website gallery.

MOUNTAIN BIKING IN THE CITY

Where can you clean gnarly trails in the middle of the city?

When people make plans to go mountain biking in Oklahoma, typically they think they need to pack up the car for a road trip to a state park hours away. While the state does boast some fantastic trails, the close-to-home answer is right on the northern end of Lake Hefner. Bluff Creek Park's west end offers a 3.4-mile, single-track dirt trail that includes switchbacks, tight turns around trees, and plenty of obstacles to tackle, including exposed tree roots and wood plank crossovers.

While the list of challenges may seem daunting altogether, the track is rated "intermediate" and a friendly ride. There are a few steep grades upwards of 8 to 10 percent to keep things interesting, but for the most part, the trail is relatively flat. This makes for a great chance to take in the natural environment with all your senses. Paying attention is crucial because the trail is also popular with hikers and people running their dogs on terrain more rugged than the paved loop around Lake Hefner.

BLUFF CREEK TRAIL

WHAT: Mountain biking fun inside the urban metro

WHERE: 11301 N Meridian Ave.

COST: Free

PRO TIP: Trails can get busy, so try to time your ride for off-hours.

Keep an eye out for wildlife such as deer and Canadian geese on the trail, as well as the brushwood huts that folks have set up.

The entry to Bluff Creek posts warnings with trail regulations.

For those wanting a longer ride, Lake Stanley Draper offers three loops of single-track dirt trails off Southeast 89th Street and Post Road on the northeast side of the lake. These trails combine for a total of about seven miles and range from easier green and blue loops to the challenging red loop. Grades run up and down much more often than at Bluff Creek with plenty of switchbacks, narrow wooden bridges, and twists to keep riders on their toes. As an added feature, riders will come across warning signs that "hitchhikers may be escaping inmates."

THE MEMORIAL FENCE

Is that original chain-link fencing at the Memorial Museum?

It is no secret in Oklahoma City that on April 19, 1995, a bomb went off at the Alfred P. Murrah Federal Building, killing 168 people and wounding hundreds more. Nor is it a secret that rescue teams from all over the country hurried to help with the recovery. But what may surprise some people is that, decades after the attack, one of the earliest monuments continues to be a part of the national memorial.

Soon after the bombing, a construction fence surrounded the site to protect it while keeping safe those who came to see the demolition. Tokens began to appear on the fence, tied into place one after the other. Some were commemorative treasures and photographs of the people who were lost. Others were more representative items of comfort and faith like stuffed animals and American flags. The fence became iconic as a place to remember always the love and efforts that came out of such destruction.

OKLAHOMA CITY NATIONAL MEMORIAL & MUSEUM

WHAT: Remembrance and education about the Oklahoma City Bombing

WHERE: 620 N Harvey Ave.

COST: $15 for adults, $13 for seniors, $12 for students

PRO TIP: According to Tripadvisor travelers, this is the #1 thing to do in Oklahoma City.

Another living portion of the memorial is the Survivor Tree, an American elm that miraculously withstood the blast. An orchard commemorating rescuers surrounds and protects it.

Inset: *"And Jesus Wept,"* a statue erected by St. Joseph Catholic Church where the Parish House stood before the bombing. Top: *The Memorial Fence is still a place of remembrance for those who passed.*

Today, a $29 million national memorial stands in the place of the lost Murrah Building. On the west end of the Outdoor Symbolic Memorial park, one section of that original fence still stands and still serves as a place of remembrance. To this day, visiting people leave gestures of love that show the lost will never be forgotten.

Next to the memorial park, the world-ranked memorial museum resides in the old Oklahoma City Masonic Temple building. The collection is packed with relics that tell the story of the bombing and the heroism that came after it. Items include banners with hopeful messages donated from across the country, the starting line from the first Memorial Marathon, and a can of Dr. Brown's Cel-Ray, part of a case that was given to a responder from New York who mentioned he would like some of the Brooklyn-born soda.

WINGS IN FLIGHT

Who were the women of aviation?

On the second floor of the headquarters of the International Organization of Women Pilots, there is a 5,000-square-foot museum that will astound anyone with aeronautical interest. Its history dates back to 1929, when 99 women pilots came together to promote aviation through education, support, and shared passion. The women had gotten to know each other through air races, including one that August before that took a week to dash between Santa Monica, California, and Cleveland, Ohio. Their first elected president was world-class aviator Amelia Earhart, and soon their numbers swelled beyond the initial 99 to thousands.

In 1955, the headquarters of the 99s moved from New York to the more centrally located Will Rogers World Airport Terminal Building. After decades of donated materials built their collections, the 99s opened their museum to the public to show the contributions of women to aviation.

In 1972, the Amelia Earhart brand of luggage became the award of choice for winners of 99s contests, which are still going strong today with scholarships for young aviators.

Top: *The Museum of Women Pilots is the first site to see upon arriving at the Will Rogers World Airport.* Inset: *Relics within the 99s museum include Amelia Earhart's teapot.*

Opal Kunz was the first president of the Ninety-Nines, this teapot was used at the first meeting on November 2, 1929 at Valley Stream, Long Island.

A tour through the Museum of Women Pilots presents an incredible century of history. Items include gloves, goggles, and flying helmets belonging to heroic women such as Amelia Earhart and Katy Stinson, the fourth woman ever to earn a Fédération Aéronautique Internationale (FAI) pilot's license.

Further exhibits show the contributions of the Women Airforce Service Pilots (WASPs), who tested and flew planes across oceans to deliver them to servicemen. Even though they were not permitted to serve in combat, women flew every single plane built for World War II.

In addition to the 99s, exhibits show other heroic women in history. A case details the story of the Night Witches, the Soviet 588th Night Bomber regiment that conducted more than 800 missions. Another display tells the story of the Mercury 13 women, including Oklahoman Jerri Cobb, who trained to be astronauts through private funds. Though their petitions were denied, they proved that women pilots could do anything men could.

BIG AIR

How did an Oklahoma kid change BMX forever?

In 1983, BMX bicycle motocross was barely 10 years old as an organized sport. So, too, was Mat Hoffman, an 11-year-old from Edmond who had come to Madison Square Garden to compete in what had been a hobby for him: ramping his bike into the air and seeing how high he could get. Hoffman later told the adventure website Mpora that he had learned the tricks on his own and "didn't have anything or anyone to reference . . . I was just doing my own thing." When he finally did see his points of reference with the others, he noted, "Woah, I guess I am going higher than everyone else."

Hoffman did and has continued to push the limits of BMX through innovation and daring. In 1993, he began the pursuit of Big Air by riding a homemade 21-foot-tall quarterpipe, double what people were usually riding. He won two gold medals in the X-Games in 1995 and 1996 and continued to place for six years while others retired. Hoffman has set and broken records, base-jumped from cliffs in Norway with his bike, and worked in film and video games to showcase what BMX riders can do. Not even 25 surgeries, including ones to remove a ruptured spleen and inflate a collapsed lung, kept him from pursuing the highest heights. It's no wonder Oklahoma City named its action sports park for Hoffman.

While not quite as tall as Hoffman's ramps, the spacious park offers 26,000 square feet of surface area for skateboards,

Hoffman was inspired to double the size of his ramp to double his speed and thus height by stuntman Johnny Airtime, who explained it was all physics and mathematics.

Top: *Bowls, rails, and pipes adorn the Mat Hoffman Action Sports Park.* Inset: *Street art decorates the concrete at the park.*

inline skates, and BMX freestyle bikes. The park is divided into sections with a street course and two bowl courses offering three shapes of panda bowl, volcano, loveseat, waterfalls, and rollers. It was listed as one of top 10 skate parks in the nation by *National Geographic* in 2009.

MAT HOFFMAN ACTION SPORTS PARK

WHAT: Biggest skate park in OKC

WHERE: 1700 S Robinson Ave.

COST: Free

PRO TIP: The park opens at dawn, so get there early to beat the crowd, or, because it stays open until 11 p.m., stick around and hang with the crowd.

MORE THAN JUST RATTLERS

Have you petted a Galapagos tortoise?

Opening the door to the OKC Rattlesnake & Venom Museum sends out a blast of hot air, just the way cold-blooded creatures like it. Founded by Carl Sandefer in 2018, the museum is a winding walkway filled with glass walls, showing some of the world's most dangerous reptiles. Sandefer, who has years of experience handling animals with the Oklahoma City Zoo in addition to a lifetime of fondness for the creatures, soon began taking in wild snakes found by others in the wild or former pets whose owners could no longer care for them.

The true drive of the museum is not only to care for the animals, but also to educate the humans who may encounter them. As Sandefer and other staff members explain, the greatest danger is not understanding which creatures will attack when fearful and which are no threats at all. Often, rattlesnakes will strike only to protect themselves. Others, such as the stubby Gaboon viper, will come after you. In addition to snakes, the museum has reptiles such as crocodiles and tegu lizards, as well as a goliath bird-eating spider. Guests can get even closer with educational programs offered throughout the year.

Not all the creatures at the Rattlesnake Museum are fearsome. Mutley, son of the OKC Zoo's Galapagos tortoise, Max, has a hay-scattered space indoors. With staff's guidance and

---

OKC RATTLESNAKE & VENOM MUSEUM

WHAT: Herpetarium with snakes, lizards, and tortoises

WHERE: SW 14th St. and S Agnew Ave.

COST: Free (buy a T-shirt while you're there!)

PRO TIP: Stay tuned to their Twitter handle, @snakemuseumokc, for special streaming shows.

Top: *There are snakes aplenty and of every variety.* Inset: *More than just rattlers hang out around the museum.*

permission, guests can feed Mutley and even pet his rough head. He's a bit of a ham and always comes back for more petting. One staff member noted that on summer days when they take him back into the yard, he just wants to soak up the sun instead of going back inside. At some 400 pounds, he usually gets his way.

Because snakes have very low metabolic rates, they can often go a week between meals. Call ahead to plan your visit if you want to catch feeding times.

THE LIGHTHOUSE

What's a lighthouse doing 500 miles inland?

When people typically picture lighthouses, it is usually atop a rocky Atlantic bluff pounded by frigid surf, but one stands proudly right in the middle of Oklahoma City. By definition, a lighthouse must be a tower serving as an aid to navigation. While there are Coast Guard navigation beacons on the Arkansas River, it wasn't until 1999 that Oklahoma gained its first real lighthouse. This stands at the East Wharf on Lake Hefner, 50 years after the lake itself was built.

Completed at the end of Mayor Robert A. Hefner's eight-year leadership in Oklahoma City, the namesake lake was a new reservoir to supply the rapidly growing population. A basin of 25,000 acres not only provided generations more drinking water, but also plenty of recreational space. Several parks circle the lake, which is famed for its jogging trails, often voted the best in the city, as well as grounds for golf and remote-control planes. The

LAKE HEFNER BOATHOUSE

WHAT: Lake fun, including boating lessons and paddleboarding

WHERE: 4407 S Lake Hefner Dr.

COST: Rent a kayak or paddleboard for $20 per hour.

PRO TIP: Dogs are welcome to go boating, too, just bring along their pup personal flotation devices.

The Centennial Lighthouse in Elk City, Oklahoma, stands proud marking 100 years of statehood, but it isn't technically a lighthouse because it doesn't overlook a navigable body of water.

Top: *The lighthouse is a functioning beacon, helping to bring in boats safely to the marina.* Inset: *The Lake Hefner Lighthouse keeps watch over the wind-choppy waters.*

Oklahoma City Boat Club, which was built in 1930 from old sailing clubs that cruised on Lake Overholser, had found a new, expansive home.

During the 1990s, the Boat Club tackled projects to improve the lake. The east end of the lake came alive with a new sea wall on the north end, expanded marinas with hoists and pads, and the old fixed docks replaced by floating ones. The most iconic addition was a 36-foot lighthouse that not only serves as a navigational beacon for sailors to get their bearings on the eastern shore but also as one of the most-photographed sites in Oklahoma City.

BIRDS OF A FEATHER

Who knew there was so much to know about pigeons?

Too many people unfortunately hear "pigeon" and think just of birds on the sidewalk, but a trip to the American Pigeon Museum will change that! It houses the extensive history of pigeons, which have been part of human society for millennia as a food source, service animals, and glamorous pets. The museum started in 1973, initially as the American Homing Pigeon Institute. Since then, it has expanded its collection through donations to become a powerhouse that teaches about the incredible birds known as pigeons.

Several permanent exhibits give new perspectives on the bird. The Homing & Fancy portion of the museum shows the *many* different breeds of pigeons, which come in all shapes and sizes, including the black-and-white Strasser, the skinny Brunner White, and the feather-footed Fairy Swallow. It also tells of the impressive navigating abilities of homing pigeons, which cross thousands of miles to get messages through. More pigeon stories come in the

Pigeons are some of the most decorated military animals. The British PDSA Dickin Medal has been awarded to a cat, four horses, 36 dogs, and 32 pigeons.

Inset: *A whole wing of pigeon paraphernalia explains the bird's many breeds and duties.*
Top: *Much of the museum is dedicated to pigeons' wartime service.*

War History exhibit, detailing pigeons' service from delivering mail in and out of besieged Paris in the Franco-Prussian War, to the use of pigeons to transport messages too secret to be broadcast over telephone lines or radio during World War I and II. The Racing exhibit shows not only the history of the sport, but also a huge collection of racing clocks, displaying how technology has evolved from timing pigeons as they compete.

The museum also serves as the home of numerous pigeons. If guests time their visits right, they might be able to see the birds as they come out for sunning. They may even get to meet a few for a petting session, to marvel at their soft, colorful plumage in a seemingly endless variety of styles.

FOUR HUNDRED FEET OF MURALS

Who's painting walls down at the Plaza?

Painted walls are the latest sight to behold in the busy Plaza District northwest of downtown along 16th Street. The area has long been a hopping feature of Oklahoma City culture. It began as a route of the streetcar system that headed toward Oklahoma City University from downtown, but the tracks never quite made it. Instead, a block along 16th Street was set up as a streetcar turnaround.

Being at the end of a trolley line was convenient, so the neighborhood flourished. In 1926, the Plaza Court became the first suburban shopping center in the city; soon after, the Plaza Theatre opened, featuring 881 seats. Hard times hit the district after World War II, turning the area into a skid row, but the neighborhood turned around with urban revitalization. Today, the Plaza is known for wide sidewalks left over from the turnaround space, curious shops, unique restaurants, and shows at the Lyric Theatre and OKC Improv. With so many things to see and do, there's a bit of a secret hiding in plain sight. Going down the alley, leading to shops behind Dig It and Bad

PLAZA WALLS

WHAT: A rotating mural project bringing alleys to life

WHERE: 1745 NW 16th St.

COST: Free

PRO TIP: Check back in from time to time for fresh art.

The Oklahoma Mural Syndicate is busy around the state with projects in Miami and El Reno, as well as the *With Love* installation in eastside Oklahoma City.

Top: *Murals wrap around the block, even decorating fences and trash bins.* Inset: *The entry to the outdoor art stands right between Dig It and the Lyric.*

Granny's Bazaar, reveals an outdoor art exhibit that will make eyes widen and jaws drop.

Launched in 2015, the Plaza Walls was a project of artists Dylan Bradway and Kristopher Kanaly, working with the Oklahoma City Arts Commission and Urban Design Commission. Managed and curated by the Oklahoma Mural Syndicate, drab brick walls burst into vibrant public art, turning an alley into a phenomenal visual experience. There are more than 30 murals from two dozen artists, giving new life to "canvases" that stretch 12 feet tall for more than 400 feet.

STAY IN A MUSEUM

Where can you take in some art on the way to your room inside a factory?

In 1916, Ford Motor Company opened a four-story assembly plant in Oklahoma City that employed 1,400 workers who churned out more than 200 Model T automobiles every day. Workers pushed their constructions along rollers on each floor, adding bit by bit as they went. At the end, an elevator system took the car down to the ground for delivery to dealerships. One of the early workers was Fred Jones, who by 1922 opened his own Ford dealership. He was an innovator in getting vehicles to people, offering services such as being open overnight and refurbishing used cars at low cost. When Ford closed its plant in 1967, Jones was quick to pick it up as his own parts distribution center for the next 46 years. Even when that closed, the building was not empty for long before the 21c Museum Hotel moved in.

Founded in Louisville, the vision of the hotel perfectly matched the revitalization of old industrialized downtowns into living spaces. The upper floors were renovated into plush, modernist hotel rooms, while the ground floor was transformed into a showcase of artwork from dozens of creators. The structurally sound manufacturing plant was incorporated into the design, with the old car elevators as light spaces and the lobby entrance in the former exit for the newly assembled Model Ts. Original ironwork still shows its stuff on the west side of the

The ground-floor museum is open for viewing when it is not used as an event space, and guests staying upstairs get extra art in the hallways between rooms.

178

Top: *An old factory gets a facelift and a new life in luxury.* Inset: *The* River of Time *flows on its conveyor.*

building at the entrance to Mary Eddy's restaurant (named for Fred Jones's wife).

Exhibits change out every 12 or so months to ensure there is always something to see, but two pieces of art are permanent additions to the hotel museum. One is the *River of Time* in Mary Eddy's that took numerous engineers and artists over a year to perfect, featuring conveyors that bring colorful shapes around to tell the time. The other is outside the entrance, a favorite of 21c cofounder Steve Wilson. *Woozy Blossom* is a metallic tree that sprays mist to keep travelers outside cool.

21C MUSEUM HOTEL OKLAHOMA CITY

WHAT: Comforts of a hotel and inspiration from art, all in a refurbished Model T production facility

WHERE: 900 W Main St.

COST: Rooms from $126/night

PRO TIP: Check out the Pet Package for some doggy spa treatment when traveling with a pooch.

THUS, ON ITS SOUNDING ANVIL-SHAPED

Where does the term "farrier" come from?

"As a shoer, you can make a million dollars with a good hammer," Lee Liles told *Shop Talk Magazine* in 2012. Liles got started in the business in 1965, crisscrossing the country with good hammers and making a name for himself in the world of horseshoeing. Along the way, he built up an impressive collection of tools and knowledge about the long history of shoeing horses, which he was eager to share with anyone who wanted to learn. Though Lee passed in 2018, his legacy lives on, not only in showing what can come of hard work, but also in a museum to showcase a growing historical collection.

The Museum of Horseshoeing Tools is packed with fascinating tidbits that one might not expect. Exhibits show the historical ties with blacksmithing and the use of many of the same tools, such as the anvil, hammer, and bellows. It goes deeply into the details of horseshoeing with the differences, such as specialty tools, and shows how farriers (from "ferrum," for "iron") needed a personality to work with animals as much as the strength to mold metal. The vivid portrayal from Longfellow's "The Village Blacksmith" is highlighted on the museum walls to show how central farriers were to life when horses were everything.

Literature exhibits provide extensive history, such as the Nature Plate scandal, which started with an "inventor" promising a great new technology that prompted capitalists to buy out his company

---

For a road trip, head down to Sulphur, Oklahoma, to see *Faithful Anvil*, a metal sculpture affixing anvils to a 24-foot cross. Each anvil bears the name of an honoree who contributed to horseshoeing.

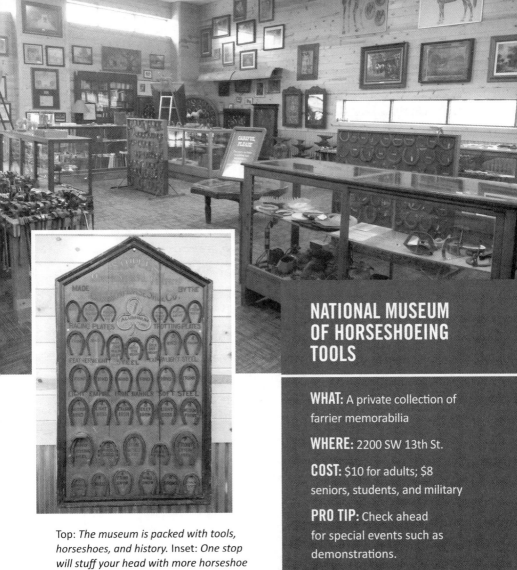

Top: *The museum is packed with tools, horseshoes, and history.* Inset: *One stop will stuff your head with more horseshoe knowledge than you would have ever thought possible.*

NATIONAL MUSEUM OF HORSESHOEING TOOLS

WHAT: A private collection of farrier memorabilia

WHERE: 2200 SW 13th St.

COST: $10 for adults; $8 seniors, students, and military

PRO TIP: Check ahead for special events such as demonstrations.

for $500,000, before it was revealed his invention was really nothing new. In fact, as the museum shows, horseshoes remained much the same for 200 years, with eight nail holes, though in all kinds of shapes and sizes for different horses and jobs. Modern views show some changes in engineering, with twice as many nail holes in the shoes, which are often made of tungsten, aluminum, and titanium alloys, in addition to the traditional iron. However, as the hoof anatomy exhibit shows, it's all about what's best for the horse.

KID NOLL

Who haunts the original Bricktown Brewery?

Bricktown has gone through many different forms as it has evolved next to downtown. Originally, it was set aside as the camp for soldiers watching over the Land Run. Then, it became the economic hub of the young territory, with the intersection of the north-south Santa Fe and the east-west Katy rail lines. It was called the Wholesale District then, since everyone would come to buy their goods wholesale from the huge brick buildings. Gradually the economy shifted, but the brick buildings stayed. Efforts to transform them into something new came to fruition with Metropolitan Area Projects Plan (MAPS) projects building a ballpark and a canal. One of the first businesses to open in the revitalized neighborhood was Bricktown Brewery in 1992, which is still going strong.

A generation before breweries sprung up around the state, the Bricktown Brewery had its kettles churning out fresh brews for customers. Combined with all-American eats, the spot in

BRICKTOWN BREWERY

WHAT: First brewery in Oklahoma

WHERE: 1 N Oklahoma Ave.

COST: Sweet potato fries with sea salt and caramel go for $3.79.

PRO TIP: Ask if the brewers are in, and they'll give a rundown of what's new on tap.

Through three decades, the Bricktown Brewery has opened numerous locations outside of Bricktown, reaching all across Oklahoma and into Texas, Kansas, Missouri, and Arkansas.

Right: *The Bricktown Brewery helped revitalize the old Wholesale District.* Inset: *Kid Noll's signature.*

Bricktown has brought in family diners to an area that once was avoided. The brewery runs straight through the building, which is decorated with original and refurbished woodwork from its old days as part of the Williams Candy Company. It even has the original company vault in the basement where profits were stored, leading to a ghost story today, as the door is infamous for opening and closing itself when no one is around.

There are plenty of other strange goings-on at the brewery, including things disappearing and turning up in odd places a week later or lights flicking on with no one at the switch. The culprit is called "Kid Noll" after his signature appeared on a beam after a reopening, marked 1918 in old-style ink. Who the Kid was is a mystery that remains to this day.

GLAMPING IN A CONESTOGA OR A TEPEE

Want to camp without really roughing it?

Few pleasures beat sitting around the campfire late into the night, swapping stories and roasting marshmallows. It gets even better when, instead of an air mattress on the ground underneath a thin tent, you can crawl into a king-sized, plush bed in the air-conditioning.

Veterinarian, insurer, and racehorse breeder Dr. Glenn Orr and his family opened the farm for activities in 2004, and it has been growing ever since. At its beginning, the farm was a chance to show a bygone era when most families made their living from the land. As the sense of community grew, the Orrs' mission to inspire real-life memories for visitors brought innovation, with carnival games and creative, home-built playground equipment. Today, guests not only enjoy the extensive petting zoo, fishing pond, and

ORR FAMILY FARMS

WHAT: Fun and educational activities right on the family farm

WHERE: 14400 S Western Ave.

COST: Book online to visit for $14; family glamping starts at $200/night.

PRO TIP: Campers get after-hours access to the farm, such as complimentary campfire s'mores!

The Orr Family Farm is packed with educational opportunities for field trips, such as learning to milk, how food gets from the farm to the dinner table, and the life cycle of a pumpkin.

Left: *A glamorous take on sleeping on the trail. Bigger wagons have bunk beds, too.* Right: *Within animal hide walls, the tepees are climate-controlled and comfortable.* *Photos courtesy of the Orr Family Farm.*

train rides, but also human foosball, giant jumping pillows, and the cannon blasters shooting gallery. As with life on the farm, everything is seasonal, making the experience unique in the spring, with baby animals, and in the fall, with harvest games.

Instead of just making it a day trip, visitors can stay on the camping grounds in larger-than-life covered wagons and authentically constructed tepees. The experience offers quite a bit more comfort than the tougher lives of pioneers on the trail and the Native Americans who followed the great herds of the plains. Modern guests have heating and air-conditioning, refrigerators, and electric lighting. The smaller wagons and tepees offer private bathrooms, complete with a shower that would've been the dream of any teamster or cowboy. In addition to the amenities in their rooms, guests receive after-hours access to the playground and swim spa, not to mention the campfire.

WALK THROUGH THE EXPERIENCE

Where can you be totally immersed in art?

Words aren't going to convey the full experience of visiting Factory Obscura Mix-Tape: nor could photos, video, or audio. It's a total journey, physical, mental, and emotional, that visitors need to experience for themselves by entering through a huge, stylized ear.

Factory Obscura came together in 2017 to drive art in the community, not just in creating but also supporting, through determining how to keep art sustainable for artists, as well as awakening the deeper potential of the audience. As more artists joined to contribute, a team of more than 30 creators assembled the Mix-Tape, a building-sized universe that conveys the experience of giving or receiving a mix-tape. Six thousand square feet are divided into several rooms, each an emotional component of the ride that goes on inside us when we listen to the musical flow.

The rooms explode with color, texture, and activities that match the emotion, whether it be Love, Angst, or Wonder. Each corner is a new experience, from a Flamingo Den show with birds rocking out, or bubbles sparkling in harmony, or a net-covered dead end to convey frustration. Visitors are encouraged to explore, such as lifting the lids of the trash cans to see critters

Mix-Tape is Factory Obscura's third installation and its first permanent one. Keep an eye out for their other experiences being created around the metro.

The eye-catching colors and forms on the front of Factory Obscura hint at what's inside.

FACTORY OBSCURA MIX-TAPE

WHAT: A handcrafted, immersive art experience by an Oklahoma City–based art collective

WHERE: 25 NW 9th St.

COST: $17 for adults, $12 for kids

PRO TIP: Every third Thursday is for ages 18+ only, for grown-ups to have the run of the place.

inside or slipping down the Infinity Slide. Even the exterior is interactive, with lights and music at the push of a button.

Each emotion also has its own embodiment in The Feels, six characters designed to show how all the pieces fit together to make our world experiences bigger and more vibrant. Stickers of The Feels and plenty of art to take home are available in the gift shop.

WHERE THE COWBOYS WATCHED THEIR MOVIES

What cinema in Oklahoma City is a century old?

In 1924, Stockyards City was hopping with cattlemen bringing in their herds to market. Along with restaurants and taverns that sprang up to give the hardworking fellers a bit of a vacation, the American Theatre opened to show silent films. It must have astounded folks from rural parts of the state who rarely had a chance to see moving pictures, and soon, even talkies. The American would go through several incarnations through the years as the Blue Moon Theatre and the Rodeo Theatre. For a stint in the early days of the 2000s, it was even an antique mall, but 2018 saw the building return to its roots as a movie house.

Working as a 501(c)(3), the Rodeo Cinema underwent significant renovations to bring back the charm of the classic film experience with modern luxuries. It has become a travel destination with broadcasts and live music in addition to the projection screen, bringing back what the theater experience had once been. Manager Sean Peel described the projection room being used as an apartment at one point, but now things are back to moviegoers getting their snacks in the same concession room as their great-grandparents did.

The Rodeo Cinema specializes in small-release films from indie creators, which is a fascinating draw but only the beginning. Much of the programming today focuses on big movie events alongside panels featuring creators and actors. Patrons come from hundreds

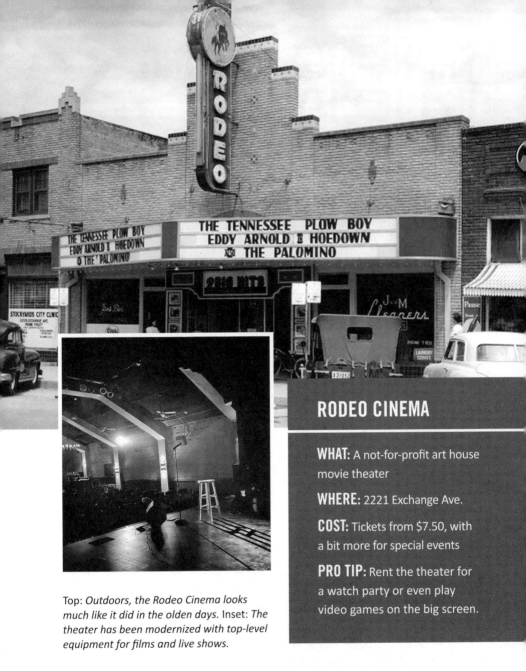

RODEO CINEMA

WHAT: A not-for-profit art house movie theater

WHERE: 2221 Exchange Ave.

COST: Tickets from $7.50, with a bit more for special events

PRO TIP: Rent the theater for a watch party or even play video games on the big screen.

Top: *Outdoors, the Rodeo Cinema looks much like it did in the olden days.* Inset: *The theater has been modernized with top-level equipment for films and live shows.*

of miles for special replays of classic films with live discussions from actors, such as Alex Vincent ("Andy" in *Chucky*) and Shaun Weiss ("Goldberg" in *The Mighty Ducks*). Outside the auditorium, fans get together for free lobby shows, including those put on by the Ernest Film Club and Alfred Hitchcock Club as well as NBA watch parties, presenting a little something for everyone, with snacks right at hand.

SKIING AND SURFING IN THE CITY

How has technology brought the slopes and waves to the plains?

Oklahoma City's long history with the North Canadian River has had numerous twists and turns. After the canal project for industry and pleasure yachting dried up in 1889, the city straightened the river to open up more land for building. In 1923, the river flooded, devastating the western side of town and leaving 1,000 people homeless. In the 1950s, the Army Corps of Engineers widened the river to ensure floods like that would never happen again. With the Metropolitan Area Projects Plan (MAPS), a $50 million system of engineered locks turned a seven-mile length of what had been a ruddy stream into the Oklahoma River. Suddenly OKC had a waterway for Olympic-level racing, but that was only the beginning.

Engineering brought whitewater rafting and kayaking to the north side of the river through a course built at the Boathouse District. In a loop with hidden upturns, ledges, and water jets, the park synthesized rapids that wouldn't be seen naturally for hundreds of miles out west, to the Rockies. Instead, they're right at home.

Technology continues to bring adventure sports to Oklahoma City with surfing and skiing. With support from Lopez Foods, the nonprofit RIVERSPORT Foundation installed a ramped

BOATHOUSE DISTRICT RIVERSPORT ADVENTURE PARK

WHAT: Outdoor urban adventures

WHERE: 800 Riversport Dr.

COST: Xtreme Season Pass starts at $125

PRO TIP: Get a group together for discounts and reservations for private parties.

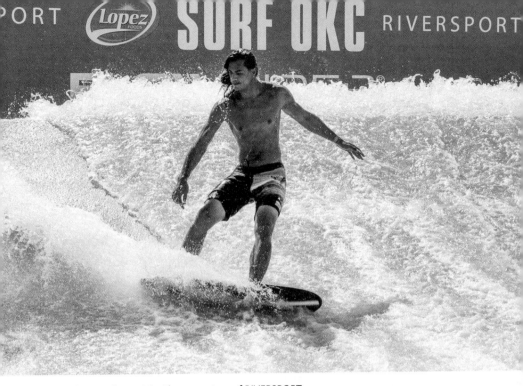

Surfing on the prairie. Photo courtesy of RIVERSPORT

device that drives a continuous stream of water on tension fabric to create an infinite wave worthy of the North Shore. The Inasmuch Foundation supported another addition with Ski OKC, a carpet of misted, low-friction fibers that rotates like a conveyor. On skis and snowboards, riders balance between gravity and science to experience gentle slopes or steep black runs, just as they would in the mountains—and without the cold! What would 19th-century settlers of the flat, broad Great Plains think of nature-simulating machines of the 21st century?

To keep the outdoors accessible to everyone, RIVERSPORT offers scholarships and free camps for rowing, sailing, and even surfing—a first for a state 500 miles inland.

GOLD-PLATED BANJOS

What museum has an upstairs nightclub?

The American Banjo Museum arrived in Oklahoma City in 2009, coming from Guthrie after needing more space to show its impressive collection. A trip through the museum begins with "370 years of banjo history in eight minutes," as the welcome desk will tell you. An audiovisual history explains how today's banjos evolved from traditional African instruments that incorporated the reverberating nature of a drum with the vibrations of strings set on a neck. Slaves produced music on homemade banjos, which came into the mainstream through the 19th century. In the Jazz Age, the banjo was the perfect instrument for lightning-fast melodies in a joyful pitch. Even the Great Depression couldn't keep the banjo down as it gained new life through musical genres such as bluegrass and folk.

From there, the museum opens up to galleries showcasing banjos that will blow away anyone with eyes to see and ears to hear. Banjo players were the rock stars of their days, with legions of followers and luxurious lifestyles that included gold-plated instruments. Visitors will be stunned to see banjos costing enormous fortunes sitting just feet from humble wood-and-hide constructs made a century before, which are priceless today.

Upstairs, the displays continue with special exhibits. A hall is dedicated to the Women of the Banjo, including Dolly Parton and Taylor Swift. Another showcase tells the story of the ukulele, the

Top: *Glass cases house examples of banjos from across the decades, even centuries.* Inset: *Practice banjos hang in the learning lounge, waiting to inspire a brand-new player or to allow accomplished pickers to show their stuff.*

banjo's relative and "America's Musical Pal," as it was nicknamed in its heyday. Most stunning of all is an event space made up like Your Father's Mustache, a nightclub chain where banjo music thrived in the 1960s and 1970s, allowing visitors to experience the thrill of a night on the town with a sing-along soundtrack.

The museum also hosts the Mark Twain Prize banjo presented by the Kennedy Center to comedian and musician Steve Martin, the inspiration for OKC's own Lucas Ross.

HOUSE ON THE LAKE

Where else can you stay in a former lodge, senator's home, or monks' residence, all in one?

Places take on different roles as the years pass, and the Monastery at Forest Lake has a winding history unlike any other. It began in 1928 as the lake lodge for the Twin Hills club to the west. On paper, it was officially a fish hatchery for the anglers association where members could meet. Legends abound about the place as a speakeasy with card games for some of Oklahoma's wealthiest oil men. A 150-pound door and a secret staircase out the back of the big parlor hint to Prohibition-era escapades.

After booze laws loosened and the need for a club dwindled, Robert S. Kerr bought the place as his personal residence, living there even during his time as governor. When he went on to be Senator Kerr in 1949, he sold the home, which continued as a private residence until it was donated to the Holy Protection Orthodox monks. Through the 1970s and 1980s, the monks were busy on the property baking bread to sell, serving as volunteer firefighters for the Forest Lake community (they all had CPR and EMS training), and raising ostriches alongside the Oklahoma City Zoo. The ostrich project evolved out of a duck rescue, which proved the monks had a knack for raising birds. To this day, a monument honors the monks for their contribution to the zoo's ostrich program by drastically improving hatch rates.

Even the range of animals in the site's history is broad, stretching from fish hatcheries to ostriches to a five-foot grass carp, often mistaken for an alligator.

THE MONASTERY AT FOREST LAKE

WHAT: 10,000-square-foot B&B and chapel on 14 acres

WHERE: 3500 N Coltrane Rd.

COST: Rooms starting for $150 per night, events for $450 and up

PRO TIP: The B&B is for grown-ups only, making it a quiet getaway just a few miles from downtown.

Top: *The red native stone of the original lodge is framed by modern brick, marrying the past with the comforts of the modern.* Inset: *Sometimes mistaken for a chimney, the "tower" is actually a water pump that once supplied the tanks for the fish hatchery.*

When the monks moved on, the monastery again became a private residence and changed hands until it came to Matthew and Sharyn Pierce, who updated it to a quaint and comfortable B&B. Today, the home offers a chance for guests to experience literal layers of history. Its wedding chapel alone hints of days as a dining room, a prayer room for monks, and a gaming parlor through the years.

ART-O-MAT AT THE CONTEMPORARY

Where can you get art from a vending machine?

Too often, when people hear "art museum," they think only of centuries-old paintings or ancient statues. Art is going strong all around us, and the Oklahoma Contemporary Arts Center is the place to take in what living creators are doing. Originally based at the State Fair Park as the City Arts Center, the nonprofit has grown to include a new installation in Campbell Park, just north of downtown, that opened in 2020. With 54,000 square feet, the museum is packed with exhibits, studios, classrooms for educational programs, and a café to keep artists fueled.

Even the Oklahoma Contemporary's building itself is a work of art. Architect Rand Elliot designed a structure of metal and glass that would reflect the sky. He told *The Oklahoman* that the building, dubbed "Folding Light," has "an ever-changing skin. On cloudy days, it will react

OKLAHOMA CONTEMPORARY ARTS CENTER

WHAT: Hotter-than-modern art showcasing today's living talent

WHERE: 11 NW 11th St.

COST: Free!

PRO TIP: Check out daily public tours to see the highlights and learn behind-the-scenes info.

Thanks to Christian Keesee and Kirkpatrick Foundation Director Marilyn Myers, admissions to exhibitions have always been and will always be free.

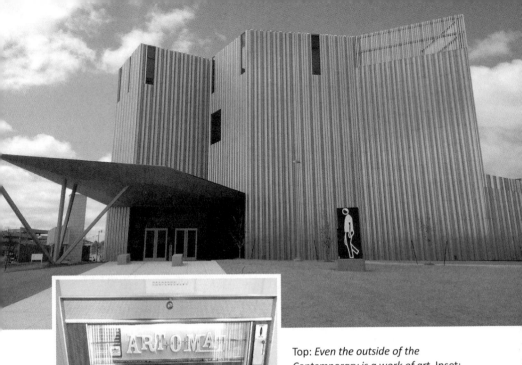

Top: *Even the outside of the Contemporary is a work of art.* Inset: *Get art at your convenience from the Art-o-Mat!*

to the gray sky, and the surface will be undulated and changing with the sun." The interior is flexible to fit traveling exhibits (the museum doesn't collect any art; it only shows it on loan from the artists), and the Te Ata Theater literally changes with an adjustable stage that can stand prominently upfront for concerts, move out into the audience for theater in the round, or recede for film screenings.

One of the must-dos at the museum is to explore the possibilities of the Art-o-Mat. Artist Clark Whittington began converting old vending machines to dispense small packages of art in 1997, and one of his unique creations has been with the museum since 2009. The Oklahoma Contemporary is the only place in Oklahoma to experience having art delivered as easily as a candy bar. After all, it is a snack for the mind!

SOURCES

The Land of the Red People—All at Once: Crum, William. "With tribe's input, the First Americans Museum Will Open Sept. 18 after a Long Delay." *The Oklahoman*. April 5, 2021. "FAM." famok.org

Washington Irving's Camp: Hoig, Stan. "Irving, Ellsworth, Latrobe, and Pourtales Expedition." *The Encyclopedia of Oklahoma History and Culture*. okhistory.org/publications/enc/entry.php?entry=IR004

Road Named for a Fort Named for a General: "Historic Fort Reno—Established 1875." fortreno.org. Phillips, Mary. "The Archivist: Despite Efforts, Street Name Remains the Same." *The Oklahoman*. June 19, 2017. oklahoman.com/article/5552875/the-archivist-despite-efforts-street-name-not-changed

The First Town in OKC: Hoig, Stan. "Boomer Movement." *The Encyclopedia of Oklahoma History and Culture*. okhistory.org/publications/enc/entry.php?entry=BO011

Making the Run: Schwab, Kyle. "Land Run Monument Briefly Site of Skulls." *The Oklahoman*. June 25, 2013.

Forty-Foot Jog: McRill, Albert. *And Satan Came Also: An Inside Story of a City's Social and Political History*. Oklahoma City, OK: Britton, 1955.

Adopt-a-Pothole: Sutter, Ellie. "Two Louisiana DJs Adopt Oklahoma City Pothole." *The Oklahoman*. January 19, 1988.

The Death of Mayor William L. Couch: Smith, Emily B. "THE STATUS OF PROVISIONAL GOVERNMENTS IN OKLAHOMA." *The Southwestern Social Science Quarterly*, vol. 13, no. 4, 1933, pp. 353–367. JSTOR, jstor.org/stable/42864834. Accessed February 4, 2021.

An Original Farm: Green, Don. "Harn, William Fremont." *The Encyclopedia of Oklahoma History and Culture*. okhistory.org/publications/enc/entry.php?entry=HA027. "Harn Homestead." harnhomestead.com

The Bricktown Canal's Predecessor: Lee, Robert E. "Downtown Canal Idea Isn't New." *The Oklahoman*. December 11, 1992.

The Golden Age of Rail: "Home - Oklahoma Railway Museum." oklahomarailwaymuseum.org

Mansion on the Prairie: "Henry & Anna Overholser Mansion." overholsermansion.org

Parks by the River: O'Dell, Larry. "Amusement Parks." *The Encyclopedia of Oklahoma History and Culture*. okhistory.org/publications/enc/entry.php?entry=AM018. "Wheeler District." wheelerdistrict.com

Baum Building: "Hillerman Map Project." Oklahoma Historical Society. okhistory.org/research/hmresults.php?mapnoinput=3h&action=Search. Phillips, Mary. "Baum Building Once Had No Comparison in Region." *The Oklahoman*. May 12, 2014.

Packingtown: "Home." stockyardscity.org. "Oklahoma National Stockyards Company." onsy.com

Oklahoma City's Oldest Restaurant: "History." Cattlemen's Steak House. cattlemensrestaurant.com/history

Going to Market: Beutler, Mark. "Memories of the OKC Farmer's Market." *405 Magazine*. August 25, 2015. "Home - OKC Farmers Market." okcfarmersmarket.com

The First Fire Station in Oklahoma: "OSFA - Oklahoma State Firefighters Association." osfa.info/museum/welcome

Forgotten Doors: "Capitol Tours." Oklahoma House of Representatives. okhouse.gov/information/capitoltours.aspx. Hinton, Mick. "Enormous, Long-Hidden Doors Discovered at State Capitol." Norman Transcript. August 4, 2015. Talley, Tim. "Hidden Door, Walled Windows among Oklahoma Capitol Mysteries." AP. January 21, 2017.

Dressed up in Trusses: "Lake Overholser Bridge." Route 66: A Discover Our Shared Heritage Travel Itinerary. National Park Service. nps.gov/nr/travel/route66/lake_overholser_bridge_oklahoma_city.html

Paddle the Wetlands: "Stinchcomb Wildlife Refuge." City of Oklahoma City Department of Parks & Recreation. okc.gov/departments/parks-recreation/parks-trails/ward-1-parks/stinchcomb-wildlife-refuge. "Stinchcomb Wildlife Refuge." Travel OK. travelok.com/ch/listings/view.profile/id.16210

The Genuine Populist: Burke, Bob. "Gore, Thomas Pryor." *The Encyclopedia of Oklahoma History and Culture*. okhistory.org/publications/enc/entry.php?entry=GO013

The Old Interurban: Loudenback, Doug. "Okc Trolleys Part 1." Doug Dawgz Blog. dougdawg.blogspot.com/2007/09/okc-trolleys-part-1.html. Loudenback, Doug. "Trolleys Part II." Doug Dawgz Blog. dougdawg.blogspot.com/2010/05/trolleys-part-ii.html. "Oklahoma City Streetcar. Love the Loops" okcstreetcar.com

Not-So-Invisible Man: "Looking at the 'Invisible Man.'" *405 Magazine*. April 6, 2016. 405magazine.com/looking-at-the-invisible-man. Taylor, Gordon O. "Ellison, Ralph Waldo." *The Encyclopedia of Oklahoma History and Culture*. okhistory.org/publications/enc/entry.php?entry=EL009

School on the Hilltop: "Home - Mount St. Mary High School." mountstmary.org. Johnson, Larry. "Early Public Schools in Oklahoma City." Metropolitan Library System. metrolibrary.org/archives/essay/2019/07/early-public-schools-oklahoma-city

Colcord: Law & Business: Wilson, Linda D. "Colcord, Charles Francis." *The Encyclopedia of Oklahoma History and Culture*. okhistory.org/publications/enc/entry.php?entry=CO020

Wild Mary Sudik: Weaver, Bobby D. "Oklahoma City Field." *The Encyclopedia of Oklahoma History and Culture*. okhistory.org/publications/enc/entry.php?entry=OK028. "World-Famous 'Wild Mary Sudik.'" American Oil & Gas Historical Society. March 24, 2013. aoghs.org/petroleum-pioneers/world-famous-wild-mary-sudik

Oil Wells at the State Capitol: Hillinger, Charles. "Petunia Has Been Good to Oklahoma." *Los Angeles Times*. August 10, 1985. Savage, Cynthia. "Oklahoma Capitol." *The Encyclopedia of Oklahoma History and Culture*. okhistory.org/publications/enc/entry.php?entry=OK080

Gubernatorial Ghost: "Governor's Mansion Welcome to Governor Stitt." governor.ok.gov/about/mansion

Film Row: "Film Row OKC." DowntownOKC. filmrowokc.com. Wynn, Bradley, and Steve Lackmeyer. "The Incredible True Story of Film Row." *The Oklahoman*. January 1, 2010.

Speakeasy Legends: Dowell, Sharon. "Former Chef Recalls Years Working at Kentucky Club." *The Oklahoman*. February 7, 1999. "Gabriella's Italian Oklahoma City." gabriellasokc.com. Hudson, Cullan. "It was Oklahoma City's Most Exclusive Night Club." Strange State. Nov 4, 2013. strangestate.blogspot.com/2013/11/it-was-oklahoma-citys-most-exclusive.html

Skirvin's Legacy: "Downtown OKC Hotels Luxury Hotel: The Hilton Skirvin." skirvinhilton.com

Strange Nights at Belle Isle: "Belle Isle Park." Metropolitan Library System. metrolibrary.org/node/44088: "Strange Light Mystifies City." *The Oklahoman*. May 3, 1924.

Dinner at O.A.'s: Nelson, Mary Jo. "Cargill Home Transformed into Restaurant." *The Oklahoman*. June 2, 1985. The Petroleum Club. petroleumclubokc.com

Riding the Rails: "History." Heartland Flyer. heartlandflyer.com/history. "Oklahoma City, OK (OKC)." Great American Stations. greatamericanstations.com/stations/oklahoma-city-ok-okc

Father of the Electric Guitar: Bob Burke, "Christian, Charles Henry," *The Encyclopedia of Oklahoma History and Culture*, okhistory.org/publications/enc/entry.php?entry=CH060: "Oklahoma Jazz Hall of Fame." okjazz.org

Dr. Haywood's Building: "The Dr. W.L. Haywood File." *The Oklahoman*. October 20, 2003. Robinett, Kerri, et al. "Oklahoma SP Haywood Building." National Register of Historic Places. August 4, 1995. catalog.archives.gov/id/86511760

The Invention of the Shopping Cart: Esparza, David. "A History of the Grocery Cart." October 20, 2018. engage3.com/2018/10/grocery-cart-history-1

The OKC Kidnapping That Made the FBI: O'Dell, Larry. "Urschel Kidnapping." *The Encyclopedia of Oklahoma History and Culture*. okhistory.org/publications/enc/entry.php?entry=UR009

The Park-O-Meter: Everett, Dianna. "Parking Meter." *The Encyclopedia of Oklahoma History and Culture*. okhistory.org/publications/enc/entry.php?entry=PA015

Neighborhood of Firsts: Beutler, Mark. "A Delectable Family Tradition." *405 Magazine*. July 25, 2013. "The Paseo Arts District." thepaseo.org. Wilson, Linda D. "Nichols, Gilbert Apple." The Encyclopedia of Oklahoma History and Culture. okhistory.org/publications/enc/entry.php?entry=NI003

Older than OKC: "Historical Churches in Oklahoma City." Universal Life Church. ulc.org/ulc-blog/historical-churches-in-oklahoma-city. "Perfect Venue for Your Special Events." Old Trinity of Paseo Oklahoma City. oldtrinityofpaseo.com

Oklahoma City's 33-Story Slide: "City Place History." City Place. cityplaceok.com "City Place Tower (Oklahoma City)." Wikipedia. en.wikipedia.org/wiki/City_Place_Tower_(Oklahoma_City)

The Thing about Our Airports: "Will Rogers Airport." WRWA. flyokc.com. "Welcome to Wiley Post Airport." WPA. wileypostairport.com

Roses under Glass: "About the Gardens." City of Oklahoma City Department of Parks & Recreation. okc.gov/departments/parks-recreation/will-rogers-gardens/about-the-gardens. "OKC – Grand Boulevard Loop." Ride Oklahoma. rideok.com/okc-grand-boulevard-loop

Hall of Famers: "Oklahoma Hall of Fame." oklahomahof.com

Home of the Thunderbirds: "45th Infantry Division Museum." 45thdivisionmuseum.com O'Dell, Larry. "Urschel Kidnapping." *The Encyclopedia of Oklahoma History and Culture.* okhistory.org/publications/enc/entry.php?entry=UR009

USS Oklahoma Anchor: Neimeyer, C.P. "USS Oklahoma." *The Encyclopedia of Oklahoma History and Culture.* okhistory.org/publications/enc/entry.php?entry=US003. "The USS Oklahoma." Oklahoma Historical Society. okhistory.org/learn/ussok. "USS Oklahoma Anchor Historical Monument." Willis Granite. willisgranite.com/content/uss-oklahoma-anchor-historical-monument

Stock Car Races and Pro Games: Carlson, Jenni. "Opinion: How Taft Stadium, 86 Years Young, Is Still Making History, Memories with Energy FC's Return." *The Oklahoman.* July 13, 2020. Lynn, Linda. "#ThrowbackThursday: Taft Stadium Stock Car Racing All the Rage in 1951." *The Oklahoman.* April 15, 2021.

The Rise, Fall, and Resurrection of Automobile Alley: "Automobile Alley." Oklahoma City Hotels, Things to Do, Restaurants & Events. visitokc.com. "Downtown in December." downtownindecember.com

The Machine Gun on Top of Byron's: Donnelly, Claire. "A Machine Gun Turret on the Roof of a Liquor Store?" *How Curious.* KGOU. November 16, 2018. kgou.org/post/how-curious-machine-gun-turret-roof-liquor-store

Milk Bottle Grocery: "Milk Bottle Grocery." Route 66: A Discover Our Shared Heritage Travel Itinerary. National Park Service. nps.gov/nr/travel/route66/milk_bottle_grocery_oklahoma_city.html. Warnick, Ron. "Milk Bottle Building Will Be Restored." *Route 66 News.* August 19, 2014. route66news.com/2014/08/19/milk-bottle-building-will-restored

Where the Stars Sing: "Civic Center Music Hall." Wikipedia. en.wikipedia.org/wiki/Civic_Center_Music_Hall. Kielty, Martin. "When Future Eagle Vince Gill's Bluegrass Band Opened for Kiss." Ultimate Classic Rock. September 28, 2020. "OKC Civic Center Music Hall." okcciviccenter.com

Leapy the Leopard: Lott, Rod. "After Escaping Zoo in 1950, Leapy the Leopard Held City in Fear." *Oklahoma Gazette.* October 4, 2007. okgazette.com/oklahoma/after-escaping-zoo-in-1950-leapy-the-leopard-held-city-in-fear/Content?oid=2960240. "Oklahoma City Zoo: Find the Explorer in You." okczoo.org

Sit-Ins against Segregation: Decker, Stefanie Lee. "Luper, Clara Shepard," *The Encyclopedia of Oklahoma History and Culture.* okhistory.org/publications/enc/entry.php?entry=LU005. Wallace, Josh. "March Commemorates Historic Oklahoma City Sit-In." *The Oklahoman.* August 19, 2018.

Showing Your Stuff: "Home." Oklahoma Sports Hall of Fame. oklahomasportshalloffame.org/home-1

Tastes of Brazil: "Café Do Brazil – Authentic Brazilian Cuisine in OKC." cafedobrazilokc.com. Coleman, Steve. "Café do Brasil, Oklahoma City, OK." okgourmet.com/ok/cafebrasilokc.html

Pei's Plan: Lackmeyer, Steve, and Jack Money. *OKC: Second Time Around.* Grass Valley, CA: Full Circle Press, 2006.

The Tunnels: Donnelly, Claire. "A Chinatown Underneath Oklahoma City?" *How Curious.* NPR. March 20, 2018.

The Great Annexation: Brus, Brian. "January 1959 Annexing Land Left Young City Room to Grow." *The Oklahoman.* April 18, 1999. "Lakes & Camping." City of Oklahoma City Department of Parks & Recreation. okc.gov/departments/parks-recreation/lakes-and-fishing. Money, Jack. "Explosive Growth." *OKC History.* October 1, 2008. okchistory.com/index.php?option=com_content&view=article&id=138:explosive-growth&catid=40:events&Itemid=77. Wilson, Linda D. "Draper, Stanley Carlisle." *The Encyclopedia of Oklahoma History and Culture.* okhistory.org/publications/enc/entry.php?entry=DR001

Skeletons!: "Skeletons: Museum of Osteology." Skeleton Museum. skeletonmuseum.com

Exotic Animal Racing: English, Mitch. "Remington Park's Ninth Annual Extreme Racing for Charity." KOKH. April 20, 2018. okcfox.com/news/local/remington-parks-ninth-annual-extreme-racing-for-charity. "Remington Park: Racing & Casino." remingtonpark.com

Wrong to Call It a "Pet Cemetery": National Cowboy & Western Heritage Museum. nationalcowboymuseum.org. Keeping, Juliana. "Final Resting Place." *The Oklahoman.* October 20, 2015.

Little Saigon: Halpern, Sue, and Bill McKibben. "Oklahoma City Is Becoming a Hotspot for Vietnamese Food." *Smithsonian Magazine.* March, 2016. smithsonianmag.com/arts-culture/oklahoma-city-becoming-hotspot-vietnamese-food-180958096. McCleland, Jacob. "How Vietnamese Refugees Spent 40 Years Rejuvenating an Oklahoma City Neighborhood." KGOU. December 30, 2015.

Sonic Booms and Sonic Cups: Borsky, Paul N. "Community Reactions to Sonic Booms." National Opinion Research Center, University of Chicago. August, 1965. Fugate, Tally D. "Sonic." *The Encyclopedia of Oklahoma History and Culture.* okhistory.org/publications/enc/entry.php?entry=SO007

Diamond Ballroom: Gowdy, Vernon L., III. *Diamond Ballroom: From Country Swing to Heavy Metal.* Yukon, OK: VGimages, 2017.

Many Miss Americas: Erwin, Robert K. "Here She Is . . ." Focus Magazine. Summer, 2003. p 4–9. McDonnell, Brandy. "'Bachelor' Host and Oklahoma City University Chris Harrison returning to emcee Miss America Competition." *The Oklahoman.* July 24, 2017. "Miss OCU Competition." Miss Oklahoma City University. missocu.com

The Legend of Little Carey: Provine, Jeff, and Tanya McCoy. *Haunted Oklahoma City.* Charleston, SC: The History Press, 2016.

Osler Building: Ambler, Cathy. National Register of Historic Places. May 2012. catalog.archives. gov/id/86511700. Farley, Tim. "Historic Osler Building Becomes Boutique Ambassador Hotel." ionOKLAHOMA. ionok.com/travel/historic-osler-building-becomes-boutique-ambassador-hotel

The Curious Case of Reverend Dolan: Farley, Tim. "Friend Says Slain Priest Target of Other Attacks." *The Okahoman.* December 17, 1988. Minty, Chip. "Priest Beaten to Death in Apartment." *The Oklahoman.* December 1, 1988. "St. Vincent's Home." Abandoned Oklahoma. abandonedok.com/st-vincents-home

Ghost Caught on Tape!: Lamkin, Virginia. "Oklahoma: Puckett's Ghost." Seeks Ghosts. April 1, 2013. seeksghosts.blogspot. com/2013/04/oklahoma-pucketts-ghost.html

Mountain Biking in the City: "Bluff Creek Unpaved Trail Loop – Oklahoma." AllTrails. alltrails.com/trail/us/oklahoma/bluff-creek-unpaved-trail-loop. "Off Road Trails." City of OKC. okc.gov/departments/parks-recreation/trails/off-road-trails

The Memorial Fence: "Museum." Oklahoma City National Memorial & Museum. memorialmuseum.com/museum

Wings in Flight: "Honoring the Past & Looking Toward the Future." Museum of Women Pilots. museumofwomenpilots.org

Big Air: Higgins, Matt. "Rider's Vision of Bigger Ramps Helps Launch Big Air." *New York Times.* July 28, 2010. nytimes. com/2010/07/29/sports/29bigair.html. Kenny, Stuart. "Mat Hoffman Interview." Mpora. mpora.com/bmx/mat-hoffman-25-years-top/#B6ISS7clwIeQkMl2.97. "Skate Parks." City of Oklahoma City Department of Parks & Recreation. okc.gov/departments/parks-recreation/skate-parks

More Than Just Rattlers: Rains-Moad, Sierra. "New OKC Rattlesnake Museum to Showcase Oklahoma's Most Dangerous Snakes." *The Oklahoman.* June 18, 2018.

The Lighthouse: "About." Oklahoma City Boat Club. okcboatclub.com/about. "Lighthouses of the United States: Oklahoma." ibiblio.org/lighthouse/ok.htm

Birds of a Feather: "Pigeon Museum." The American Pigeon Museum. theamericanpigeonmuseum.org

Four Hundred Feet of Murals: "Historical Streetcar Routes OKC." Association of Central Oklahoma Governments. acogok.org/transportation-planning/maps-and-data/historical-streetcar-routes. "Plaza Walls." plazawalls.org. "Plaza District." plazadistrict.org

Night in a Museum: "Art Museum, Hotel & Restaurant." 21c Museum Hotels. 21cmuseumhotels.com/oklahomacity. Fugate, Tally D. "Fred Jones Manufacturing Company." *The Encyclopedia of Oklahoma History and Culture.* okhistory.org/publications/enc/entry. php?entry=FR009. Lackmeyer, Steve. "Historic Register Application Shows Oklahoma City Plant's Close Ties to Ford Motor Co." *The Oklahoman.* May 3, 2014.

Thus, on Its Sounding Anvil-Shaped: Museum of Horseshoeing. horseshoeingmuseum.com

Kid Noll: "Come and Get It." Bricktown Brewery. bricktownbrewery.com. Lackmeyer, Steve. *Bricktown.* Mount Pleasant, SC: Arcadia Publishing, 2009.

Glamping in a Conestoga or a Tepee: "Orr Family Farm." orrfamilyfarm.com

Walk through the Experience: "Factory Obscura." factoryobscura.com

Where the Cowboys Watched Their Movies: "Rodeo Cinema." rodeocinema.org, "Rodeo Arthouse Cinema in Oklahoma City, Oklahoma." Cinema Treasures. cinematreasures.org/theaters/2543

Skiing and Surfing in the City: "RIVERSPORT OKC." riversportokc.org

Gold-Plated Banjos: "American Banjo Museum." americanbanjomuseum.com

House on the Lake: "The Monastery at Forest Lake: Wedding Chapel." themonasteryatforestlake.com, Posey, Ellie. "Monastery Tends to Its Ostriches." *The Oklahoman.* May 6, 1982.

Art-o-Mat at the Contemporary: "Art-o-mat." artomat.org. Lackmeyer, Steve. "The Downtown Future Home of Oklahoma Contemporary Arts Center Will Feature Four-Story Building." *The Oklahoman.* June 14, 2015.

INDEX